'Finally, a book that understands not just the theory of collaborative learning but also understands how to roll its sleeves up and make it happen. I really enjoyed Nick's book. He breaks down the blueprint of collaborative learning and how to overcome typical challenges. This will be a benefit to anyone who reads it.'
Danny Seals, Co-founder, Venndorly

'Nick's passion for collaborative learning shines through; that provides energy for the reader! There are some excellent case studies which provide a good context for the thinking.'
Andy Lancaster, Head of Learning, CIPD (The Chartered Institute of Personnel Development)

'As Nick Hernandez points out in *Collaborative Learning* (chapter 2), the non-conscious nature of knowledge, per the research of Richard E Clark, EdD, is the challenge, especially for High Stakes Performance. If the risks and rewards at stake allow it, iterative and collaborative means for developing information and instruction are almost always better, faster and cheaper than most L&D organizations' approaches.'
Guy W Wallace, President, EPPIC Inc

'One barrier to changing how learning is delivered is quantitative justification that the change will solve critical business problems. Nick has pulled together a comprehensive guide defining what collaborative learning is, why it matters, and exactly how this dynamic change will have a measurable impact on some of the most critical problems keeping business executives up at night. He does all this while artfully highlighting 360Learning only when it ties directly to the role it has in making collaborative learning a reality. I also appreciate his sincere recognition that making the change comes with challenges while providing practical guidance on overcoming those challenges.'

Christopher Lind, Founder and Principal Adviser, Learning Sharks/Learning Tech Talks

'In L&D, books that stick are the ones that simply answer the question, "how do I make this work in my organization?". Nick absolutely nails this in his guide to collaborative learning. It's filled with well-researched thinking, real-world examples and obstacles that learning professionals may face when trying to implement this approach within their business. I found myself continually flicking back to how collaborative learning can be applied to different stages of the employee journey, and how it enhances culture. It is smart, incredibly practical and nuanced, providing me and my team with plenty of ideas to put into action. This is a must-read book that not only challenges the status quo but that L&D professionals can rely on to inspire them to make stuff happen.'

Adam Harwood, Associate Director of Talent and Culture, Biotechnology

'Something's always sat wrongly with me in professional and corporate L&D. It has felt overly programmatic and formulaic. Enter Nick Hernandez and this book. All the chapters are well researched, storified and practical. This book is culture enhancing and spark inducing. We've been waiting for this work without truly knowing so, and from now on, all learners stand to gain when you apply the urges, tools and approaches contained here. I'd lost faith in learning, it's now restored.'

Perry Timms, Founder and Chief Energy Officer, PTHR

'Collaborative learning is one of the defining characteristics of high-performing learning organizations – talked about by many but practiced by few. It's time for action! I'd echo Nick's own advice in this book – pick it up, use the ideas in the case studies and stories, test them, experiment with them and see what works!'

Laura Overton, award-winning L&D analyst and Founder, Learning Changemakers

'Nick makes a strong case for the power, the impact and the absolute necessity of collaborative learning in today's increasingly digital and remote workplaces. Yesterday's top-down learning approaches no longer serve our businesses or employees. It is well past time to put learners in the driver's seat of their own performance and development, and collaborative learning does just that.'

Bob Mosher, CEO and Chief Learning Evangelist, APPLY Synergies

Collaborative Learning

*How to upskill from within and turn L&D into
your competitive advantage*

Nick Hernandez

Nick

KoganPage

First published in Great Britain and the United States in 2023 by Kogan Page Limited

2nd Floor, 45 Gee Street	8 W 38th Street, Suite 902	4737/23 Ansari Road
London	New York, NY 10018	Daryaganj
EC1V 3RS	USA	New Delhi 110002
United Kingdom		India
www.koganpage.com		

Kogan Page books are printed on paper from sustainable forests.

© 360Learning, société anonyme, 2023

ISBNs

Hardback	978 1 3986 1055 2
Paperback	978 1 3986 1052 1
Ebook	978 1 3986 1054 5

British Library Cataloguing-in-Publication Data
A CIP record for this book is available from the British Library.

Library of Congress Cataloging Number
2023000256

Typeset by Hong Kong FIVE Workshop, Hong Kong
Print production managed by Jellyfish
Printed and bound by CPI Group (UK) Ltd, Croydon CR0 4YY

CONTENTS

Foreword

Powerful, memorable, impactful: How upskilling from within drives better learning

The world is moving fast. Skills are moving faster.

Back in 2019, I wrote about the power of collaborative learning to help organizations everywhere leverage their most valuable asset of all: internal expertise. I noted how our skills-based economy was driving an incredible change of pace in the way we learn – a change of pace that has since become even more frantic. Back then, companies everywhere were trying to keep up with this environment by amassing bigger and more complicated libraries of learning content, and trying in vain to reskill their workforce through sheer volume. It was a pure numbers game: if we have a big enough library, then we can't help but drive the right skills and stay ahead of the competition – or so said the conventional wisdom.

Yet, despite this mad flurry to build more content, we always seem to forget one key thing: the most powerful, memorable and impactful learning occurs when we talk with other people. We need human interaction to sit at the very heart of every great learning experience, from the classroom through to the boardroom, from the factory floor through to the showroom. That's why collaborative, cohort-based learning is the most valuable and useful way to develop new skills. It has to be approachable, and it has to be visible. It has to be human.

In other words, the learning experiences that drive real improvements to performance are defined by expert collaboration with our peers. It doesn't matter how deep or comprehensive our learning libraries may be; if we aren't harnessing, transmitting and celebrating peer expertise at every step from course creation and delivery through to iteration and measurement, then we're missing the mark when it comes to developing the skills we need to survive. And in such a competitive environment, missing the mark could put us on the fast track to obsolescence.

Of course, this focus on peer learning is far from new. I've been writing about expert-driven content since the early 2000s, when we termed it 'from e-learning to we-learning'. And even if this cute piece of terminology didn't find a foothold right away, the fundamental concept certainly did. In recent years, organizations as diverse and as influential as Google and McDonald's have significantly stepped up their efforts to harness valuable knowledge and know-how within their ranks and turn this knowledge into a competitive advantage. This way, whether they're delivering search results or flipping burgers, they're channelling their collective expertise to help every one of their people to pursue a shared goal.

When we're in a race to attract, nurture and grow the most skilled talent in the market, our ability to turn internal expertise into a real competitive advantage can make or break us. Rather than just relying on external learning content and hoping for the best, we need to empower expert authors to create content, share it, and generate an ongoing collaborative experience for their teams. This concept is the same fundamental premise behind Capability Academies – places where people can go to advance the business capabilities they need to thrive. Instead of relying on vast libraries of faceless or dull learning content, Capability Academies are sponsored by business leaders, and these senior figures decide what capabilities – the proprietary combination of skills, knowledge and experiences employees need to succeed within their company – are most important. This is more than a bunch of courses; a Capability Academy is focused on building real business capabilities in a scalable, transparent way, and driving real, sustained improvements in employee performance through iteration and peer feedback.

This fundamental shift to empowering your teams with human-centred learning experiences has never been more critical for business.

That's because, today, leaders everywhere are being asked to consider the skills their organizations will need one year, two years or even five years down the track. As we all know, the frantic pace of change has rendered classic skills matrix exercises irrelevant; by the time we've mapped everything out and planned ahead for the resources we'll need, the earth has already shifted under our feet. But if we can reorient this question to focus more on capturing, leveraging and sharing our internal expertise, we can help our teams upskill from within and stay ahead of whatever the world has in store.

This is why 70 per cent of all training in your company can – and should – come from your own people, not from professional teachers or instructional designers. When you 'unlock' these subject-matter experts to build content, you can create compelling human-centred learning experiences. More than that, you can create an environment of collaborative learning, where people can declare their learning needs and call on the power of the group to help address those needs with tailored peer-driven content. They can identify and celebrate the creators around them, and they can play their own part in building great learning content by contributing their own insights, knowledge and expertise. This way, you can help people throughout your organization upskill from within through the power of collaborative learning.

All it takes is the right blueprint.

Josh Bersin
February 2023

1

The courses you loved vs the experts you know

The shift from top-down learning to upskilling from within

A strong learning culture is one of the most important determinants of an organization's success. A business that learns effectively is better equipped to innovate and respond to challenges than one that struggles to develop and adapt its thinking and its practice. This is hardly a controversial idea. But it's easy to forget when you're busy managing your department, initiatives and programmes. The issues that arise from inadequate learning and development can be ignored for months – maybe even years. Then one day you'll wake up and realize that the cracks in the system have burst open and your organization is struggling to merely stay afloat. You may find yourself wondering how this could have happened when the answer has been staring you in the face the entire time.

Here's the thing: *We all know that learning is essential for a healthy organization.* But not nearly enough companies are having the critical discussions about the ways they learn and how their learning practices can be improved. Instead, most organizations select a learning platform, develop some courses for their entire organization and move on. Clearly, organizations recognize the importance of learning, but this 'set-and-forget' approach can have far-reaching unintended consequences including lost talent, low employee engagement, slow or non-existent innovation and limited competitiveness in the marketplace.

The reality is that the world has undergone a profound change over the past decade and the old ways of organizational learning are no longer sufficient. The rise of remote work, evolving media consumption habits and patterns of online social interaction, changing worker demographics and new technologies have all placed new demands on organizations that require dynamic new approaches to creating and sharing knowledge.

Collaborative learning offers an antidote to today's learning and development dilemmas. Collaborative learning is a training methodology where employees share their knowledge and expertise, teaching and learning from one another at the same time. But in order to effectively implement a collaborative learning environment and help people upskill from within, it's necessary to understand what it is replacing and why. In this chapter we'll explore current approaches to learning and development, their limitations, and how companies can leverage experts within their organization to drive learning success.

The courses you loved

Before we dive in, take a moment to reflect on your experience with learning and development (L&D) programmes in the past. Regardless of whether you worked at a high-growth tech startup, a chain restaurant or a multinational conglomerate, your learning experiences probably had a lot in common. Before your first day, you may have been given a packet of onboarding materials that you were expected to teach yourself prior to starting. Perhaps your first week was a blur of training sessions led by a member of the human resources (HR) team and a few other new hires. This gave you a flavour of what your learning and development experience would be like throughout your tenure at the company. New training sessions and course requirements would appear on your calendar out of nowhere and many of them had no obvious connection to the challenges you faced in your day-to-day work. The training sessions that were led by an instructor – sometimes in person and sometimes online – always happened in real time so you had to figure out ways to squeeze them into your packed work schedule. But the e-learning sessions that you had to complete in your own time weren't much better. You found it hard to pay attention during the training sessions because the course material felt irrelevant. Even if you enjoyed some of the training, when you returned to work after a session you struggled to put the lessons to use. The videos and quizzes that were optimized for 'engagement' were boring and seemingly endless. When the training concluded, you almost immediately forgot everything you were supposed to have learned.

If your experience sounds at all like the description above, it is because it is a typical one. Most of us have had learning experiences that are delivered without a sense of what the learner actually needs – and even when we might happen to enjoy the courses themselves, we struggle to put the content into practice. Almost everyone in the workforce is accustomed to these kinds of top-down and prescriptive learning experiences that resemble a typical school classroom. In many organizational L&D programmes, peer interactions are kept to a minimum, and to the extent that they do occur they are generally scripted and designed to elicit a certain response from the participants. The tools used to deliver learning or training content may differ between organizations, but their fundamental approach to pedagogy – and lacklustre results – are the same.

Of course, it's not only in-person approaches to collaborative learning that are deficient. Applying L&D solutions at scale requires learning technologies, but learning technology has been shown to have notoriously low engagement. It's almost impossible to justify the considerable investment in platforms and content suites in terms of the actual value that is delivered to an organization.

To understand why investments in learning technologies over more than three decades haven't delivered more for organizations, it's important to take a step back and explore their conception and evolution, which are largely based on the premise of the 'self-directed learner' as a motivated individual alone in a platform with generic content. Indeed, there are five key L&D technologies that are critical to understanding the dilemmas facing organizational learning today:

- learning management systems (LMS)
- learning experience platforms (LXPs)
- talent suites
- learning platforms
- Sharable Content Object Reference Modules (SCORM)

Some of these technologies have been under development for decades. Others have been around for only a few years. The boundaries that separate them are permeable and there is a lot of overlap in terms of functionality. By exploring the contexts that birthed these technologies and the problems they were meant to solve, we can readily see how our understanding of organizational knowledge management has evolved and why new tools are required to facilitate learning in modern organizations.

PCs and the birth of asynchronous learning

All modern L&D technologies can trace their origin to asynchronous learning networks (ALNs), a concept that emerged in the early 1980s alongside the personal computing revolution. The basic promise of ALNs was that digital computers would decouple education from time and space by allowing learners to interact in virtual classrooms. For the entire history of education prior to the arrival of ALNs, students and their teacher had to be in the same place at the same time. There were workarounds, of course – books allowed experts to transmit their knowledge across generations and early postal networks carried information across vast distances – but these solutions were slow and cumbersome. The most effective learning involves fluid interaction between teacher and student, and prior to the late 20th century this always occurred face to face.

The personal computer (PC) revolution changed everything. A decade before the birth of the World Wide Web, computer scientists and educational researchers recognized the incredible opportunity to use networked computers to transform the way we learn. The main benefit of ALNs was that they created more opportunities for students to interact with teachers each week because the students had the convenience of being able to 'attend class' anytime and anywhere. Students could learn at their own pace and on their own schedule.

The first experiments with ALNs were launched in colleges across the US in the 1990s and showed immense promise. During one early study on e-learning in an undergraduate economics course, students praised the new online learning system for adding flexibility to their school schedule and providing a source of feedback while learning new concepts. Many highlighted the importance of the social aspects of the program – particularly the ability to post supportive comments for other students – for keeping them engaged. 'It makes you feel like there's someone out there and you're not sitting all alone,' one student reported after the experiment. Another agreed: 'It takes away the isolation of distance education... and the interaction with the computer has actually brought us together both from an education point of view and probably socially as well.'[1]

Still, the shortcomings of virtual classrooms were readily apparent. One of the biggest issues was a lack of bandwidth. During the dial-up era, ALNs were extremely limited in terms of media richness, which circumscribed the resources teachers could draw on for their lessons and had a dampening effect on student engagement.[2] Another issue was student frustration with waiting an unpredictable amount of time for feedback. It may seem unusual in our era of constant push notifications, but at the time there was no way for a student to know when a teacher had responded to their work.[3] The only way to know was to get online and check.

The first versions of ALNs weren't perfect, but by the end of the 1980s it was already clear that they would have a prominent role to play in the future of higher education. Even though the technology wasn't quite ready for mass adoption yet, most researchers believed it was only a matter of time until the kinks were ironed out. And it would happen far sooner than anyone expected.

The e-learning boom – and bust

ALNs entered the 1990s as academic research projects and exited the decade as the darlings of Silicon Valley. There were two main catalysts for this astonishing glow up. First was the birth of the World Wide Web in 1993. These standardized protocols that defined how data was shared across the internet made this previously obscure technology suddenly accessible to millions of people who didn't know the difference between a BBS (bulletin board system) and a listserv (prototypical email software). The second factor was the dot-com boom that started a few years later. Investors began pouring capital into software startups intent on disrupting industries as far afield as banking and grocery delivery. Importantly, the dot-com boom was accompanied by massive investments in bandwidth capacity to deliver these new services to the hordes of people coming online for the first time. Between the mid-1990s and the early 2000s, hundreds of thousands of miles of fibre optic cable were laid throughout the United States.[4]

It didn't take long for the dot-com entrepreneurs to set their sights on education. By the late 1990s, there were several startups working on ALNs, which were now lumped under the larger umbrella of 'e-learning' platforms. Most took the obvious path and developed e-learning products designed for primary and secondary education. But a few saw an opportunity to move this technology into organizations that weren't explicitly institutions for education. Corporate e-learning platforms had the potential to be a wildly lucrative new frontier, but entering this market required entrepreneurs to get creative about overcoming entrenched resistance to new approaches to organizational knowledge management.

Knowledge management is the catch-all term for how businesses share information across the organization. It is, in short, the (in)formal system that describes how a business learns. There are three core components to any knowledge management system: an information repository, a network of communities, and the experts who are members of those communities.[5]

The information repository is like the Library of Alexandria. It's where all the knowledge accumulated over the lifetime of the business is kept for reference by current and future employees. The information repository could be an electronic database or some file cabinets in the basement. The form matters less than the function, which is to allow employees to access information that is relevant to their role within the organization.

The network of communities is essentially the structure of a business that can be described with an organizational chart. It shows both the structure of individual departments (HR, sales, engineering, and so on) as well as how those departments relate to one another. Each department may very well be made up of several sub-communities that are either permanent (departmental leadership) or ad hoc (a team formed to tackle a specific project).

The third and final element of a knowledge management system is the experts within the organization. These individuals have unique skills that are valuable to the functioning of the business. Some of these skills may have been specific to the organization and can be acquired only after a long tenure at the company. These are experts in the organization itself. Other experts bring valuable outside knowledge into the firm. These are subject-matter experts whose knowledge was typically gained through formal education or training.

Each component of a knowledge management system exists in every business. But that doesn't mean that every business has an effective learning system. The primary challenge for business leaders and L&D professionals is to figure out how to get each of these components to interact seamlessly. An organization with a knowledge management system where documents are collecting dust in a basement, communities are siloed and experts never share their insights with their peers is leaving an immense amount of value lying on the table. Building an effective learning culture is never easy, but as we'll see throughout this book, the businesses that prioritize learning across their organization enjoy an immense competitive advantage and a rich internal culture.

Until the e-learning boom in the late 1990s, the knowledge management systems at most businesses were painfully analogue. The most forward-thinking business had already transitioned to electronic information repositories, but other aspects of organizational learning were firmly grounded in metaspace. New employees were onboarded with scheduled orientation sessions and new processes were introduced at mandatory company-wide meetings. There were a lot of inefficiencies in this approach to learning, but there was even more institutional inertia. This was the way things had always been done and the mantra in the C-suite was 'If it ain't broke, don't fix it.'

The new generation of e-learning pioneers had their work cut out for them selling into a market so staunchly resistant to shaking up the status quo. While some companies enjoyed limited success, most collapsed when the dot-com bubble burst. In retrospect, the problem was painfully obvious. Although some organizations did indeed adopt these new e-learning technologies, they didn't actually change the way that learning occurred in their organization. They used the same training materials, the same course structures, and the same measurements of success that they were using before. As so many software entrepreneurs discovered the hard way, putting an analogue process online doesn't necessarily make it better. When the dot-com bubble burst, most e-learning companies went bust. By the time the dust settled in 2002, *Information Week* offered a sober and succinct post-mortem: 'From customer to analyst to investor, the consensus is that e-learning still has a few things of its own to learn.'[6]

E-learning grows up

Despite the failure of many first-generation e-learning companies, the dot-com boom pioneered many of the platform features that are still prevalent in digital learning systems today. The technologies forged during the heady years around the turn of the millennium ultimately determined how organizations would use digital and networked technologies to facilitate learning for the next two decades.

SCORM

The most prominent legacy of the first e-learning boom was a technical standard for creating and sharing educational media known as Sharable Content Object Reference Modules or SCORM. The standard came out of the US Department of Defense, which aimed to improve interoperability and distributed learning across public and private organizations. The diversity of e-learning software made it challenging for companies to tap into the vast libraries of educational material that were being churned out by third-party production studios. A course that worked well on one platform might not work at all on another. SCORM was built to be a solution to this problem.[7] It acted like a *lingua franca* between different learning platforms and unleashed a torrent of educational content that corporate L&D departments, in the words of one commentator, 'purchased by the bucketful'.[8]

SCORM was successful insofar as it did enable organizations to share learning materials regardless of the software they happened to be using. But this was only possible due to the creation of a cottage industry dedicated to producing the educational content for these organizations. Creating a training course in SCORM is an arduous process that can take upwards of six months and cost tens of thousands of dollars. The process begins with intensive instructional design, where course producers work with an organization to establish the goals of the content they'll be producing. Next comes the storyboarding phase, where third-party designers work with the company to establish the narrative structure and tone of the animated course. Once this groundwork is complete, animators will spend several months using sophisticated tools like Adobe Photoshop to bring the course to life.

SCORM is very much a product of its time. Today, most media on the web is structured with HTML5, but when SCORM was released Adobe Flash animation was the dominant multimedia format on the web. As a result, SCORM was built for Flash animations, which meant that the majority of e-learning courses also had to be developed with Flash. Unfortunately, the reign of Flash was short-lived.

The rise of smartphones and other mobile technologies – which don't play well with resource-intensive media formats like Flash – sounded the death knell. In 2010, Steve Jobs wrote his infamous 'Thoughts on Flash' memo that outlined why Apple wouldn't support this format on its mobile devices.[9] In 2015, YouTube, by then the world's largest video streaming platform, announced it would stop streaming videos in Flash by default in favour of HTML5.[10] The final nail in the coffin came from Adobe itself shortly thereafter, which announced it would stop supporting its own Flash Player by 2020.[11]

Although the abundance of educational material created with SCORM was well received at its inception, this standard ultimately became a millstone around the neck of future e-learning platforms. The fact that SCORM was built around Flash means that the vast libraries of educational content look as outdated as Disney's hand-drawn animations in the age of Pixar.

But the limitations of SCORM go far beyond aesthetics. Courses built in SCORM also lack much of the functionality that we've come to expect from web applications, like bookmarks, starred reviews or commenting capabilities. And because SCORM courses are so labour intensive to make, this also means they rarely get updated once they're produced. Given their long production timelines, many of these courses are already outdated by the time they are delivered. SCORM is ultimately a one-way street: courses are conceived and built by a small group of leaders in an organization with little to no feedback from internal experts and are delivered to learners who are unable to meaningfully engage with the course material. This not only makes these courses dull, it also undermines the learning process itself.

Given the many drawbacks of SCORM, you may be surprised to learn that it is still by far the dominant format for e-learning course materials today. In fact, some media producers boast libraries with more than 10,000 SCORM courses available for purchase! The reason SCORM remains so widely used can almost entirely be attributed to the sunk cost fallacy. After two decades of creating SCORM courses, there's simply too much content for L&D professionals to feel comfortable abandoning the format entirely, even when far superior solutions exist. With each passing year, we are only becoming more reliant on this outdated technology. But as we'll see later in the book, there's a way for L&D departments to keep SCORM without diminishing their organization's capacity to learn.

Learning management systems

No discussion of SCORM would be complete without a foray into the world of learning management systems (LMS). These are the software platforms that host the SCORM courses and serve as the primary interface for learners. A wide variety of LMS have been developed over the past two decades, but they tend to share several core features. A typical LMS is a web-based platform that can combine offline and online learning tasks, measure training outcomes, integrate with other software tools used by an organization, automate some administrative tasks relevant to learning, like scheduling or course registration, and host third-party educational content that learners can engage with in a 'self-serve' manner.[12]

In some ways, an LMS is what the early pioneers of e-learning had in mind in the 1980s when they dreamt of the future of asynchronous learning networks. An LMS can host a variety of multimedia, educate an arbitrarily large group of learners at their own pace, tailor content to specific groups within an organization, like the sales department or compliance office, and effortlessly track the progress of learners.

But with the luxury of experience, we can now see that many of the purported benefits of an LMS actually limit an organization's ability to facilitate learning. Consider the content hosted on these platforms. Because LMS are mainly built to host SCORM courses, much of the content that arrives on these platforms may already be stale by the time users can access it. In a dynamic organization, any learning content is bound to have a short shelf life as the business itself grows and evolves. The problem is that an LMS doesn't offer an easy way for learners to flag outdated content for the L&D team, and even if it did it wouldn't be much help because of how resource intensive it is to produce SCORM courses. As a result, anyone who uses the LMS is likely to be learning from outdated material that no longer meets the needs of the organization.

The back end business logic of a typical LMS is flawed, too. These platforms are built around a highly centralized administrative structure where an organization's L&D team are the ultimate arbiters of what occurs on the platform. They set permissions, determine what content is available and for whom, set course schedules and so on. This is by design. A centralized and compartmentalized structure hampers learning insofar as it eliminates agility in the content creation process and learner curiosity that leads to further exploration. Instead, it is designed to make it far easier to measure and control the learning process because all the members of an organization can be placed in neat, predetermined boxes. In fact, this is a prerequisite for implementing the automated administrative processes – certification, scheduling, measuring – that are a major selling point for L&D teams.

If you're like me, a learning management system that prioritizes measuring the outcomes of learning over learning itself seems entirely backward. But this isn't a bug in the software; it's a feature. The core problem with a modern LMS is that it is built for the L&D managers, not the people who will actually be using the system to learn. The back end of the system works phenomenally, but the front end is extremely limited in terms of helping an organization learn. I'm hardly the first person to recognize the shortcomings of LMS. There has been a tremendous amount of effort in the e-learning sector to improve the user experience on these platforms, but this was about as effective as putting lipstick on a pig because it didn't really improve learning outcomes.

Learning experience platforms

The rise of social media over the past decade forced many LMS providers to rethink the ways they delivered their content. As people became accustomed to the social feeds and sleek user interfaces that have become hallmarks of Web 2.0, it became painfully obvious that LMS had to get with the times or risk even more disengagement from learners. (And with course engagement levels so low, there wasn't much left to lose.) These trends led to the rise of learning experience platforms or LXPs, which sought to overcome the limitations of LMS with modern approaches to the user experience.

Initially, some legacy LMS providers tried to integrate timelines or feeds into their product in an effort to generate the same levels of engagement that social media companies like Facebook and Twitter were seeing from their users. The idea was to allow learners to post questions relevant to their needs directly into the LMS timeline and get answers from their peers in real time. It was an intuitive direction for an LMS, but ultimately turned out to be the wrong one. The problem was that these feeds didn't really lead to collaboration that results in real learning because this required embedding peer interactions within a specific activity. By mimicking an approach similar to Facebook and Twitter instead of something closer to Reddit, Stack Overflow, or even a Google Doc, these LMS reformers merely created a stream of unrelated questions and answers where relevant information was hard to find. In many cases, the LMS platform devolved into a stream of conversations that had nothing to do with learning because the timeline had no context. It was something, but not necessarily better than nothing.

LXPs, by contrast, mostly scrapped the timeline idea and instead focused on finding better ways to deliver content. A hallmark of LXPs was that they integrated educational material from a variety of sources. In addition to the SCORM courses, the new LXP systems allow L&D teams to build educational programmes that included resources from other educational outlets, whether that be a TED talk on YouTube or a massive open online course (MOOC) hosted on a site like Coursera or Udemy.

But the real innovation with LXPs was the way they helped learners find relevant content. They aimed to become the Netflix of learning platforms and took more than a few pages out of the streaming giant's playbook. This meant leaning heavily on machine learning algorithms to recommend educational content to users that would, in theory, help further their skills and career. The problem is that these platforms simply didn't have access to the user data they needed to make their artificial intelligence (AI) recommendation systems very useful. Whereas Netflix can train its AI on personal data from hundreds of millions of users, companies and their employees are much more guarded about handing over that kind of information to an e-learning company. Sure, they could build an amazing AI recommendation system for their educational content, but good luck convincing the rank and file that forking over access to their calendars, performance reviews, geolocation data and more is worth the trade-off.

While LXPs certainly made learning platforms nicer to look at and easier to navigate, they floundered on the same rocks as LMS. By focusing on content delivery, LXPs didn't really move the needle in terms of helping organizations and their members learn. There was more content, but dismal engagement. There were smarter recommendations, but they didn't lead to smarter employees. When it comes to learning experience platforms, it's mostly about the experience – the learning almost seems like an afterthought.

Talent suites and learning platforms

Despite its name, a learning experience platform isn't really a platform. It's more of a feature set that is included in either a talent suite or a learning platform. Talent suites are software that is built primarily to enable career advancement and reskilling within an organization. Their features can vary widely, but they typically include an LXP and/or an LMS along with skill analytics, succession planning, talent marketplaces, and other similar tools. Talent suites are particularly useful for HR departments in organizations with thousands of employees because they help plan and manage skill distribution and employee career trajectories at scale.

Learning platforms, by contrast, are typically 'point solutions', which means they are designed to cover particular needs for a specific customer profile. Many learning platforms are built for individual departments within an organization – such as sales or finance – but increasingly they are designed to serve organizations of any size in their entirety. Like talent suites, learning platforms include LMS and/ or LXP features. But they differ in a few crucial respects. First, they enable L&D teams to create custom content internally with minimal training because they don't require SCORM compliance. Second, learning platforms tend to focus on features that enable collaboration between employees and departments within an organization. As we'll see in the next chapter, this emphasis on collaboration is key and is the reason why collaborative learning platforms are poised to radically reshape the way organizations learn.

The experts you know: The shift to upskilling from within through collaborative learning

The big takeaway from our brief tour of core e-learning platforms, features and standards is that the choice of L&D technologies matters less than *how* they are used. For example, LXPs slapped a modern interface on top of SCORM-based content. This Netflix-like interface felt familiar and even gave users the sense that they were directing their own learning by being able to choose content from a large library. It's flashy modern tech, but the fundamental nature of the learning experience didn't change – it was still a top-down approach to learning controlled and bottlenecked by a small group of decision makers within the organization. The opportunity for learners to contribute and add further value was limited and courses were updated only sporadically. The LMS has a natural tendency to become a graveyard for outdated content.

It's as if most platforms available today totally missed the lesson from the e-learning shakeout during the dot-com boom: new technologies implemented in broken learning systems don't help people learn. In fact, in many cases – perhaps most – they will merely entrench the broken system and make it harder to fix in the future. Technology can certainly help organizations improve L&D, *but only if organizations realize that existing platforms undermine effective learning methods in their efforts to deliver L&D at scale*. A new approach to facilitating collaborative learning in an organization is necessary because nearly all learning platforms available today are not optimized for effective knowledge transmission.

A second problem with current approaches to organizational learning software is that each solution only partially meets the requirements for a robust learning system. A LMS or an LXP can act as a learning repository, but most of their content is created by third parties and collated into libraries full of irrelevant content that is difficult to update after it is created. This significantly limits its effectiveness as a learning, upskilling and reskilling tool. While some e-learning technologies flirted with building features like social feeds to engage communities within an organization, individual communities are still largely operating within their own silos. The beautiful thing about networks – in learning systems or elsewhere – is that the more people that are added to the network, the stronger it becomes. When learning software sequesters communities on the platform, it blocks the flow of knowledge and weakens the organization as a whole. Finally, most learning software doesn't allow organizations to leverage their most valuable assets – their own employees. Experts within an organization are rarely consulted by the L&D teams responsible for sourcing the content that lives on these platforms, nor do they have the opportunity to take the reins and create their own learning material to share with their peers. This is an astounding waste of talent and knowledge.

Ultimately, all of the learning platforms discussed above were marketed as *the* solution for companies that wanted to address their skills gap problem and prepare their workforce for the challenges and opportunities of the future. LXPs thrived by putting a nicer interface on the clunky LMS catalogues they were meant to replace. They made it easier to search internal and third-party content, and added some intelligent functionality to ensure the platform recommended the right course to the right person at the right time. Although LXPs did succeed in terms of improving the user experience, their dream of using AI to improve the upskilling process fell flat, as did attempts to leverage AI on LMS and talent suites.

The idea was that AI could understand the current skill needs of the company by using data such as open and current job descriptions, workforce planning documents and similar inputs, and continually update the platform to find people with the right skills and automatically recommend career paths for existing employees that could help overcome the company's skills gap. The problem was that this kind of functionality requires an enormous amount of data and technical know-how. While the large talent suites may have had the right data to make the AI systems viable, they lacked the machine learning expertise to effectively implement it. Instead, they bought AI systems from startups that lacked the data to make these programs effective. The net result was that the AI systems integrated into LMS, LXP and talent suite platforms fell far short of the capabilities these companies dreamt of creating.

The sad state of organizational learning software is no one's fault. L&D professionals have always had to make the best of the solutions that are available to them, even though they often result in a substantial administrative burden. No L&D department *chose* SCORM, but all of them were forced to use it. And because these platforms measure success in terms of course completion rather than learning or business impact, it means that L&D pros have to spend an increasing amount of their time on low-value-add tasks like ensuring all employees have conducted a particular training session. Every minute they spend doing admin work is less time they have to focus on their core responsibility: helping their organization get smarter by lowering the barriers to actual learning and the benefits it creates for individuals and the organization as a whole.

It's clear that something has to change. Today, the average course completion rate on a given learning platform is around 20 per cent.[13] This is a problem because learning and development consistently ranks among the most important factors influencing employee retention. A recent survey asked employees to gauge the importance of learning and training opportunities in their overall job satisfaction on a scale of 1 to 100. The median score was an astounding 84 and rose to 92 for employees in the prime of their career (ages 35–54).[14] Since that survey was published, Americans have left their jobs at record-breaking rates.[15] In the face of the so-called Great Resignation, it's more important than ever for organizations to develop learning programmes that propel their employees to new heights and make it more likely that they'll stick around.[16]

The only way to move beyond the dismal results from the past two decades of e-learning technologies is to use learning software that guides and supports employees to improve their performance and get more reliable results. This learning software will accomplish this by empowering employees to learn from and share their own knowledge with their peers. The new generation of collaborative learning tech removes the barriers to knowledge transmission across an organization by making it easy for anyone to create and engage with educational content. This builds a robust information repository that reflects real-time changes in the needs and direction of an organization. Collaborative learning technology abolishes the artificial barriers that separate individuals and communities in an organization who are using the same platform to foster cross-departmental dialogues that lead to real learning and innovative insights. And most importantly, collaborative learning tech puts an organization's own experts front and centre. Indeed, the 'experts you know' are the linchpin of all collaborative learning technologies. They carry the knowledge required for other employees in an organization to thrive, creating a learning environment where their expertise can be shared is key to an organization's success.

Collaborative learning is a bottom-up philosophy in a top-down world. Just the idea of such a radical shift in an organization's L&D strategy is enough to make many executives sweat. But many of the most successful companies in the world have already embraced the core tenets of collaborative learning within their organization to help their teams upskill from within.

Consider the fast-food giant McDonald's, which trains tens of thousands of new employees across its restaurants every year. Creating and sharing knowledge at this scale is an immense challenge. The company's learning system must be tailored both to the volume of new employees and to their diversity of backgrounds, which means developing course materials in different languages and that reflect a variety of cultural sensibilities. As a result, McDonald's has relied heavily on collaborative learning techniques to meet the company's L&D goals and help employees advance their careers. For example, McDonald's launched its Archways to Careers mobile app in 2020, which functions as a learning platform for employees to explore potential careers while receiving support and guidance from their peers in the company.[17]

McDonald's is just one of the organizations that have leveraged the power of collaboration and their own experts to supercharge their learning culture. The collaborative learning revolution is well underway and can be seen in organizations ranging from early-stage startups to household-name multinationals. Throughout this book, we'll have the opportunity to meet several of them and see what collaborative learning looks like in action.

Notes

1 E Stacey. Collaborative learning in an online environment, *Journal of Distance Education*, 1999

2 R Daft and R Lengel. Organizational information requirements, media richness and structural design, *Management Science*, 1986, 32, 554–71

3 S Hiltz. Collaborative learning in asynchronous learning networks: Building learning communities, US Department of Education, 1998

4 C Hogendorn. Excessive (?) entry of national telecom networks, 1990–2001, NET Institute Working Paper No. 03–7, 2004

5 M Rosenberg (2012) *Beyond E-Learning: Approaches and technologies to enhance organizational knowledge, learning, and performance*, John Wiley & Sons, Hoboken, NJ

6 Information Week. E-learning struggles to make the grade, *Information Week*, 9 May 2002, www.informationweek.com/it-life/e-learning-struggles-to-make-the-grade (archived at https://perma.cc/BPV5-5DTZ)

7 L Ananatharman (2012) Knowledge management and learning: eLearning and knowledge management system, *2012 15th International Conference on Interactive Collaborative Learning (ICL)*, 1–6

8 M Rosenberg (2012) *Beyond E-Learning: Approaches and technologies to enhance organizational knowledge, learning, and performance*, John Wiley & Sons, Hoboken, NJ

9 S Jobs. Thoughts on Flash, Apple.com Internet Archive, 2010, https://web.archive.org/web/20170615060422/https://www.apple.com/hotnews/thoughts-on-flash/ (archived at https://perma.cc/2NU8-D84Q)

10 I Paul. So long, Flash! YouTube now defaults to HTML5 on the Web, PCWorld, 2015, www.pcworld.com/article/431524/so-long-flash-youtube-

now-defaults-to-html5-on-the-web.html (archived at https://perma.cc/9JJG-SWAJ)

11   Adobe Communications. Flash and the future of interactive content, Adobe Blog, 2017, https://blog.adobe.com/en/publish/2017/07/25/adobe-flash-update#gs.ctytij (archived at https://perma.cc/2BGE-ENL4)

12   L Ananatharman (2012) Knowledge management and learning: eLearning and knowledge management system, *2012 15th International Conference on Interactive Collaborative Learning (ICL)*, 1–6

13   360Learning. Reactions: Deliver engaging and up-to-date courses with collaborative learning, nd, https://360learning.com/blog/reactions/ (archived at https://perma.cc/C9R7-4AHJ)

14   360Learning. What do your learners really want? nd, https://360learning.com/ebook/employee-engagement-survey/ (archived at https://perma.cc/8CQF-RK9L)

15   US Bureau of Labor Statistics. Quits levels and rates by industry and region, seasonally adjusted, 2022, www.bls.gov/news.release/jolts.t04.htm (archived at https://perma.cc/2EUH-JQLK)

16   I Cook. Who is driving the great resignation? *Harvard Business Review*, September 2021, https://hbr.org/2021/09/who-is-driving-the-great-resignation (archived at https://perma.cc/3BPQ-9H2L)

17   McDonald's Press Center. McDonald's launches app to help restaurant employees explore careers that match their skills and interests, 2020, www.prnewswire.com/news-releases/mcdonalds-launches-app-to-help-restaurant-employees-explore-careers-that-match-their-skills-and-interests-300990630.html (archived at https://perma.cc/QKG9-3NAL)

2

The collaborative learning blueprint for upskilling from within

Picture this: after years of grinding with a small team, a startup finally found its product-market fit and hit escape velocity. Their customer count was growing at a breakneck pace and the company had just received a fresh round of funding from a group of blue-chip investors. The founders knew that their team was about to multiply and they needed a way to get new employees up to speed as soon as possible.

This startup didn't have any formal L&D processes in place because of its small size. In the past, new employees learned the ropes through one-on-one engagements with their peers, but this solution wouldn't scale. Since the founders didn't have time to set up a formal onboarding process before their hiring blitz, they decided to ask a few of their most experienced employees to create and manage training materials for new hires on their team. The idea was to convert the information from their one-on-one ad hoc training into one-to-many training materials that new employees could use for mostly self-directed training.

The founders didn't place any restrictions on the format of these training materials. Their only requirements were: (1) new hires should be able to easily provide feedback and ask questions about the material; (2) the material should be easy to update based on this feedback; and (3) the resource must be user-centred in the sense that it would communicate how it would help new employees do their jobs, rather than just providing them with information. The founders hoped these minimal standards would ensure that training materials always reflected the true workflows and priorities of the company while minimizing the amount of time their most experienced employees had to spend training others. After a few days of work, each of the teams at the company had created their own training materials for new hires. The engineering team made an internal wiki about the company's codebase, the sales team created a series of instructional videos about how to sell the company's product, and the customer support team created FAQs in a Google Doc that covered common issues. The result was phenomenal. New hires quickly learned new information and how it applied to their role, which helped the startup quickly onboard new hires who rapidly gained proficiency at their jobs.

Whether they knew it or not, these founders had created an onboarding and training process founded on upskilling from within through collaborative learning. This is a bottom-up approach to education originally developed in the 1970s that is driven by the needs and experience of the learners themselves. Although it has since been shown to be one of the most effective and engaging methods for creating and sharing knowledge, collaborative learning was relatively unknown in the business world until recently. There were both social and technological challenges that collaborative learning had to overcome that we'll explore in more detail later in the book, but many of the world's most dynamic companies are now embracing collaborative learning to help their organization respond to challenges and opportunities in a rapidly changing world.

Collaborative learning turns the conventional approach to knowledge transfer within an organization on its head. L&D systems based on collaborative learning are the antidote to the shortcomings of modern learning platforms. It is a constructive approach to knowledge creation, which means that all learners participate in the process instead of just passively consuming information from an authority.[1] This improves learner engagement and knowledge retention while reducing the costs and administrative complexity associated with operating an effective learning system. In this chapter we'll explore the origins of collaborative learning, examine how it improves on other modes of learning, and conclude with a four-step blueprint for establishing a collaborative learning culture in any organization.

The basis of upskilling from within through collaborative learning

There are three main modes of learning: transmission/reception, individual and collaborative.

Transmission/reception learning

Transmission/reception learning is the style of knowledge transfer that most of us are deeply familiar with because it is characteristic of learning in schools and organizations throughout the world. In this arrangement, knowledge transmission is unidirectional from a teacher to their students, who have little to no say in the content or process of learning. As educational researchers have noted, this style of learning is 'grounded in a worldview that supports the teacher as authority, knowledge as a commodity, and the learner as an empty or nearly empty vessel'.[2] This is the system adopted by most learning management systems and the L&D departments that use them.

Individual learning

Individual learning is also familiar to anyone who has ever taught themselves a new skill. It is an approach to learning where the learner largely determines the knowledge that is relevant to their goals as well as the process for learning it. Like transmission/reception learning, the student is still dependent on some authoritative source of knowledge such as a textbook or online lecture. The primary difference is that the learner typically has little to no interaction with a peer group or an instructor. In the context of an organization, this typically involves an L&D department providing new hires or employees with a packet of educational materials they are expected to consume outside of a formal training session.

While there are clear benefits to individual learning insofar as the student can create their own curriculum and dictate the pace of their coursework, this comes at the cost of valuable feedback from an expert or other learners. In most organizations, the majority of learning doesn't occur out of the context of the work being done. New hires may independently engage with onboarding materials initially, but the overwhelming majority of their learning occurs on the job and learners receive feedback through their performance. This creates an incredible opportunity to introduce learning methodologies that help individuals overcome challenges they face day to day on the job.

Collaborative learning

In research on collaborative learning, this approach is typically defined as involving elements of both transmission/reception and individual learning, but is arranged in such a way that it creates additional benefits for learners that aren't found in other styles of learning. In a collaborative learning environment, learners and teachers work together in a group to produce knowledge together. Although the teacher typically does have more expertise than any of the learners, their role is to facilitate learning between the students rather than directly transmit it in the top-down fashion that is a hallmark of transmission/reception learning. Collaborative learning dismantles the traditional hierarchies in education because it doesn't necessarily privilege the knowledge of any individual in a group. All learners bring something to the table and benefit from the insights of individual peers and the group learning process as a whole. Rather than prescribing solely external resources, learners and teachers can work together to share their collective knowledge and upskill from within.

Figure 2.1 shows how bottom-up, collaborative learning compares to traditional top-down learning.

FIGURE 2.1   Top-down vs bottom-up learning

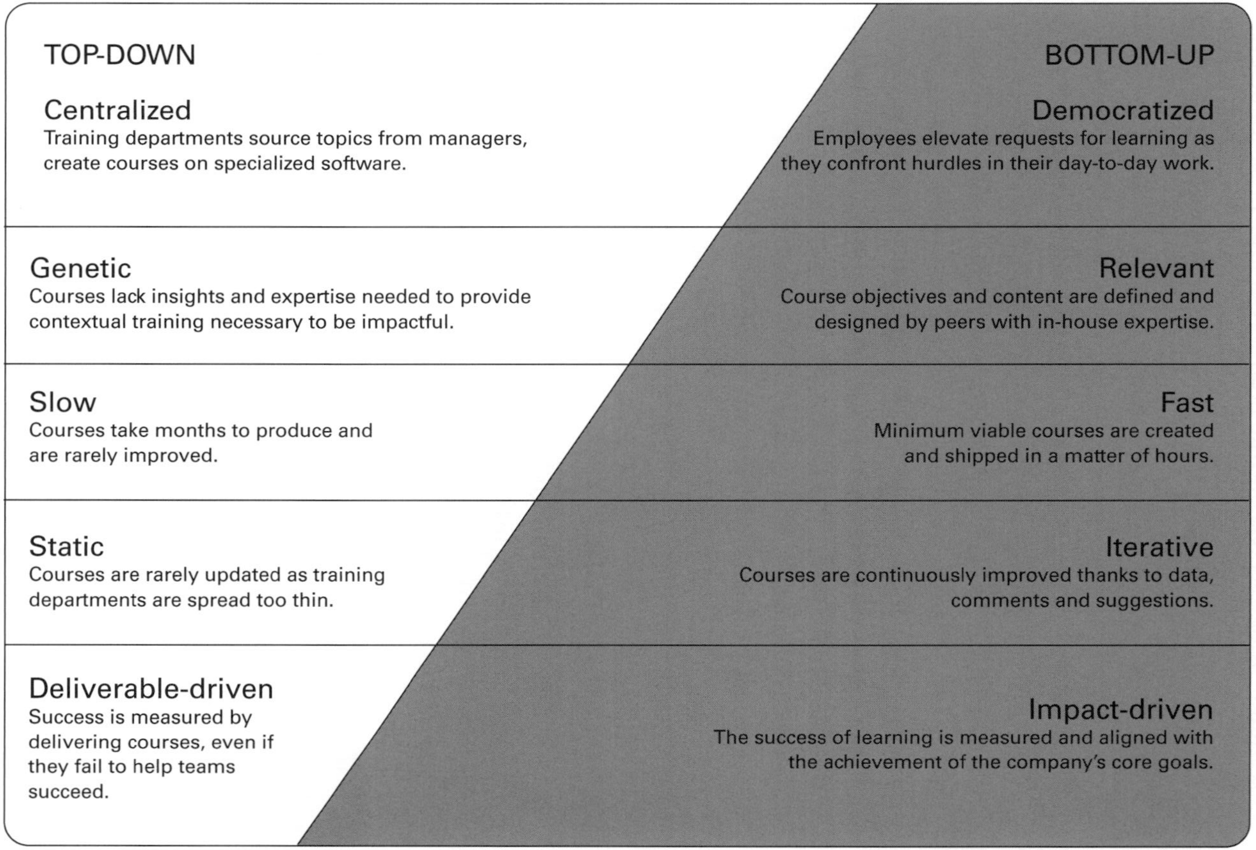

TOP-DOWN	BOTTOM-UP
Centralized Training departments source topics from managers, create courses on specialized software.	**Democratized** Employees elevate requests for learning as they confront hurdles in their day-to-day work.
Generic Courses lack insights and expertise needed to provide contextual training necessary to be impactful.	**Relevant** Course objectives and content are defined and designed by peers with in-house expertise.
Slow Courses take months to produce and are rarely improved.	**Fast** Minimum viable courses are created and shipped in a matter of hours.
Static Courses are rarely updated as training departments are spread too thin.	**Iterative** Courses are continuously improved thanks to data, comments and suggestions.
Deliverable-driven Success is measured by delivering courses, even if they fail to help teams succeed.	**Impact-driven** The success of learning is measured and aligned with the achievement of the company's core goals.

Collaborative or cooperative learning?

Although 'collaborative learning' and 'cooperative learning' are often used interchangeably, they are fundamentally different approaches to knowledge creation. They are easy to confuse because in both collaborative and cooperative learning students work in groups to create knowledge. The key difference is in how the learners relate to each other and to the problem space. In cooperative learning, each participant is responsible for solving a particular part of a given problem and these individual parts are eventually combined to produce a solution. This division of labour is absent in collaborative learning. Instead, learners coordinate with each other to solve a problem together. Individual learners must declare their own learning needs while simultaneously working with their peers to help them learn in order to create the knowledge the group needs to solve a problem. As a result of this arrangement, learners in a collaborative environment are both more self-reliant *and* more mutually dependent than cooperative learners, which makes it easier to scale across an organization.[3]

A small caveat is necessary here. As most L&D leaders know all too well, if you ask employees what their learning needs are they will typically respond by listing topics and classes. Yet, in most cases this is not what they need to really improve their performance and make progress in their career. A top-down approach to L&D analyses and aggregates requests to identify training opportunities. Yet this doesn't really account for where L&D will be the most successful. Instead, L&D leaders need more data from evidence-based practice. When employees are faced with data showing less-than-optimal performance, they will be better equipped to articulate their true learning needs. Collaborative learning programmes can help with this by collecting contextualized data to help learners identify their weak spots.

Collaborative learning was developed in the context of childhood education in the late 1970s and grew to become a major area of educational research over the following decade. It soon made inroads into higher education, and researchers working on asynchronous learning networks soon recognized that collaborative learning could be a major boon to computer-mediated education. While the 'anytime, anywhere' nature of online learning clearly held promise, by the late 1990s it was also apparent that it wouldn't be sufficient to simply transport old styles of learning onto the web.

Collaboration tools

In 1998, a group of educational researchers noted that 'one of the potential negative effects of online courses is the loss of social relationships and a loss of the sense of community' that are typically present in physical learning environments. As such, the researchers concluded that 'collaborative learning strategies are necessary in order for World Wide Web-based courses to be as effective as traditional classroom courses'. They imagined a world where increased broadband access 'afforded greater opportunities for collaboration' and opened the door for 'exciting possibilities such as synchronous shared workplaces and two-way audio-visual communication'.[4]

Today, many of the 'exciting' collaboration tools envisioned by these researchers two decades ago are commonplace. We use chat applications like Slack to create shared virtual workplaces and video platforms like Zoom to replicate face-to-face interactions between people who may be on opposite sides of the world. In other words, we're already intimately familiar with the enormous benefits that collaborative digital technologies can bring to an organization. But relatively few organizations took the next step and implemented collaborative technologies into their L&D strategy – we'll explore why in greater depth in Chapter 8 – which means they're missing out on the incredible opportunities that come from capitalizing on how people learn best.

There were some notable exceptions, of course. In the mid-2000s, a number of large companies including Intel, Motorola, Pixar, IBM, SAP, Sony Mobile and Nokia began experimenting with internal wikis as a proto-collaborative learning platform. Today, most of us are familiar with Wikipedia, the global open source web encyclopedia that allows anyone to contribute information on any topic. Corporate wikis function in a similar way, but are limited to cataloguing information relevant to the company's operations. Although other rudimentary collaborative learning technologies existed at the time, companies were attracted to internal wikis for their simplicity and convenience. It was easy to keep the wikis updated with the latest information and anyone in the organization could quickly learn how to contribute. Wikis also facilitate the flow of knowledge across an organization by allowing anyone to access any department's wiki.

While they proved to be an effective knowledge management platform, wikis were lacking in the user interface department. Missing were many of the features we now expect from modern e-learning applications, such as the ability to host rich multimedia content, take quizzes, collaborate on projects, or easily and visibly provide feedback on course material. In general, one of the most glaring problems with wikis was that they could only tell you what the wiki creator knows. They don't categorize this information in the context of situations and challenges that are faced by the individual reading the wiki who needs this information. In his research, Richard Clark, the pioneer of cognitive task analysis, discovered that master performers are not conscious of up to 70 per cent of what they do in the context of their work, which means they are not able to easily recall and share their knowledge.[5] This makes wikis incomplete at best and not particularly useful for sharing know-how and insights with others. Still, corporate wikis revealed the deep need for collaborative learning tools and their incredible effectiveness at managing knowledge creation and transmission in organizations. It was only a matter of time until more sophisticated tools appeared on the scene and took collaborative learning to the next level.

The virtues of upskilling from within through collaborative learning

Why do we collaborate? It's a deceptively simple question that is still an area of active debate among scholars who study collaboration among individuals and organizations. The answer often depends on the specifics of the collaboration, but in general it seems that people and institutions collaborate to reduce complexity and uncertainty.[6]

This is possible because successful collaborations can produce solutions that are greater than the sum of their parts.

Consider the nature of collaboration in the context of a complex project like building a house. This requires people with a wide variety of expertise – plumbers, electricians, carpenters and so on – to exchange knowledge and learn from one another to accomplish their objectives. Could an electrician and a plumber work together to build a house all on their own? Probably. But it would be an arduous process and the resulting structure would likely be highly biased toward the priorities of their respective fields. A house that is all pipes and wiring is hardly a desirable place to live. It is only through the exchange of knowledge between a diverse group of peers with a common goal and varying skill sets that a great house can be built. The same is true for learning.

Collaborative learning leverages the unique experiences of everyone within an organization, and the benefits of this approach are enormous. In the 1980s, one of the pioneers of collaborative learning enumerated 50 social, psychological and academic benefits of collaborative learning compared with conventional education methods. I'll spare you the full list here, but it's worthwhile to consider a few of the key benefits of upskilling from within through collaborative learning in what I've come to call the DESIRE framework (see Figure 2.2):

- **Democratization:** Collaborative learning democratizes education by empowering everyone in an organization to contribute to the learning process by suggesting learning needs and creating the educational content to fulfil those needs. This makes employees feel more engaged, focused and valued. The beauty of this approach is that it is structured like a fractal and can be deployed at any scale across the organization, whether it's the entire company or a sub-departmental team.

- **Speed:** Collaborative learning enables an organization to move fast and stay nimble by allowing people to come together to declare their own learning needs and convene teams to quickly create learning content to answer urgent questions. This is a radical departure from old learning systems that take months to go from idea to execution for any given course.

- **Impact:** Collaborative learning is ultimately about creating and sharing knowledge and know-how within an organization. While this is the goal of all learning systems – at least in principle – most were built so L&D teams could measure success in terms of the number of courses shipped and completed by employees. This offers low visibility into whether or not those courses actually facilitated learning. Collaborative learning, on the other hand, solicits feedback from learners who are active in the knowledge creation process, which gives a clear indication of whether a course is successful in its objectives.

- **Relevance:** One of the most significant benefits of collaborative learning is that it guarantees that courses are always relevant because employees are directly involved with identifying and fulfilling their learning needs. This means employees are more invested in the learning process and eliminates the headaches for L&D teams who must guess at employee needs and then source content to meet those needs from third parties. As the management guru Peter Drucker explained, 'There is one thing that needs to be said loudly and clearly: trainers need to realize that things are going on that don't fit their assumptions, their own training backgrounds, and the way they have been typically doing their jobs.'[7] Collaborative learning takes the guesswork out of course creation.

- **Iteration:** An organization is always striving to improve itself, which requires a learning system that can keep up with constant change. Collaborative learning tools are explicitly designed to make it painless to update courses to reflect new information or flag outdated material. This is a significant departure from previous learning systems where it was difficult or prohibitively expensive to frequently change course materials, which also lacked simple mechanisms for learners to flag outdated information to the L&D team.

FIGURE 2.2   The DESIRE framework

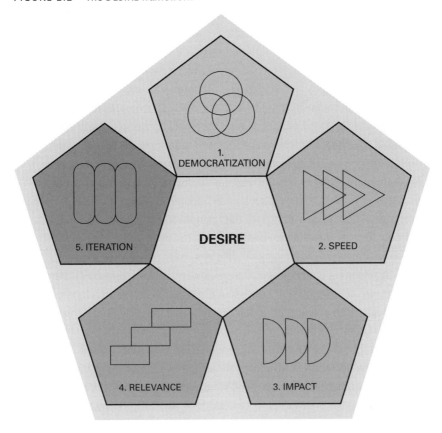

CASE STUDY
How AlphaSights leveraged its experts to fuel a digital learning transformation

Founded in 2008, AlphaSights is a platform that connects companies with industry experts to drive better business outcomes. Today, AlphaSights has more than 1,500 employees around the globe, which creates unique training needs that conventional learning platforms are ill-equipped to handle. In late 2019, the company began to transition to digital training in order to give new employees greater flexibility while enabling the company to scale its operations and measure the impact of its L&D programme.

AlphaSights knew it needed a platform that would empower any of its employees to create new courses with ease. At the same time, the learning system would need to enable AlphaSights employees to collaborate with its internal community of subject-matter experts in a seamless and scalable way. This requirement for a considerable amount of internal content led AlphaSights to adopt 360Learning as its core learning platform, and within a year its decision to embrace collaborative learning tools was already showing results.

As the global Covid-19 pandemic took the world by storm in early 2020, AlphaSights was forced to test its collaborative learning tools in a 'live fire' environment when all of its global team went fully remote almost overnight. To facilitate onboarding in this unusual environment, AlphaSights recruited its subject-matter experts to develop a blended online/in-person two-week learning programme where about a quarter of the material would be delivered in a digital-only format. This exercise demonstrated the power of leveraging internal expertise to achieve key learning goals like efficiently onboarding new employees in a rapidly changing environment. Unlike conventional learning tools that require months to develop new courses, AlphaSights was able to adapt its training programme in a matter of days while simultaneously improving the results of its training programme.

An important feature of digital collaborative learning tools is their transparency, which allows L&D professionals to have better insight into the outcomes of learning programmes. And what AlphaSights saw was astounding. By democratizing the creation of its L&D content, AlphaSights was able to launch around 27 new courses a month on average, with roughly a quarter of its employees authoring new digital training material. These courses had a 95 per cent completion rate and, based on the in-course reactions of employees, it's not hard to see why. A full 97 per cent of the reactions were positive, which indicated that new employees found the training materials relevant and useful. At the same time, 98 per cent of those trained through collaborative learning reported that it effectively prepared them for the demands of their job.

AlphaSights' decision to shift the way knowledge was created allowed the company to weather an unprecedented historical event while ensuring that employee and organizational learning needs were always being met. That's the power of leveraging internal experts and enabling peer-to-peer knowledge creation.

The collaborative learning blueprint

It's hard to say no to those kinds of benefits. But what differentiates a successful implementation of collaborative learning from one that fizzles? This question has been central to research on collaborative learning from the very beginning. In the early 1990s, David and Roger Johnson, two brothers who laid the foundation of our scientific understanding of collaborative learning, identified five conditions that must be present for this approach to learning to be more successful than other approaches.[8]

First, learners must have a positive perception of their interdependence with other learners; if they feel that collaborating with their peers is a nuisance, a successful collaboration is unlikely to occur. Second, there must be plenty of opportunities for learners to provide feedback, motivation and constructive criticism of their peers. Third, each learner must feel some level of personal responsibility for helping the group achieve its learning objective. Although no individual is solely accountable for the success or failure of the group, it is essential that everyone actively participates for collaborative learning to occur. Fourth, learners should make frequent use of interpersonal skills like managing conflict or open communication because collaborative learning depends on effective interactions between individual members and the group as a whole. Finally, learners should regularly assess the functioning of the group to identify areas where its effectiveness could be improved.

Although the Johnson brothers' research occurred in the context of educational institutions, their insights apply to any organization assessing their collaborative learning strategy. But we're getting ahead of ourselves here. Most vendors selling learning platforms to organizations tell them that they must overhaul their organization's current learning culture to create a culture that is receptive to the idea of collaborative learning before they can assess whether the conditions for successful collaborative learning are present. Transforming the way an organization creates and shares knowledge is a daunting task for any L&D professional, but fortunately this perspective is a myth. Rather than shuffling processes around and seeking permission for change, L&D leaders should instead focus on outcomes and work backwards to identify ways to achieve desired results. This ensures they are focusing on real problems in the learning culture and over time this will result in a wholesale change in the way employees learn. My experience of working with hundreds of companies who have taken this plunge revealed that there are four key steps that L&D leaders can take to build a collaborative learning culture at their organization and ensure that it is addressing real learning needs in the organization. I call it the collaborative learning blueprint.

Step 1: Embrace decentralized learning

One of the most notable achievements of the internet is how it has enabled decentralization in previously unimaginable contexts. This can be seen in processes that are both digital (peer-to-peer file sharing, cryptocurrency) and physical (remote work, swarm robotics). Decentralization can be a tricky concept to pin down precisely, but I think it helps to visually contrast it with a centralized system. One way to imagine a centralized system is as a wheel, where individual spokes radiate from a central hub. Each spoke has contact with the hub and the two spokes adjacent to it on the rim, but doesn't have a direct connection to any of the other spokes. A decentralized system is more like a spider's web, where any point on the web can conceivably be connected to any other point and there is no clear 'centre' that connects all the points.

Decentralization has many advantages: it makes a system more robust because it doesn't have any single point of failure; it alleviates the workload for any particular node in a system by spreading it across all the nodes; it enables more efficient decision making because multiple decisions can occur in parallel across the network rather than being forced to go up and down a single hierarchical chain; and it makes it easier for a network to grow because any node in a decentralized system can be a point of connection for a new node.

Despite the benefits of decentralization, many companies have been reluctant to adopt it as a principle for their own organization. In most cases, this is due to fears that come with a perceived lack of control in a decentralized organization. But time and time again, these fears turn out to be overblown. A great example of this was years of hand wringing in the C-suite over the rise of remote work. But when the global pandemic hit in 2020, remote work became the default for many companies almost overnight and the productivity apocalypse that many executives expected never materialized. In fact, in many industries productivity *increased* as more workers went remote.

Today, many L&D teams are comparably fearful about the decentralized aspects of collaborative learning. A hallmark of collaborative learning is that all employees actively participate in the learning process by identifying their learning needs, requesting and creating courses and other resources, and giving feedback on existing learning materials. This bottom-up approach overturns the conventional approach to organizational learning where L&D teams often speak to leaders and managers to elicit the learning needs of their team members, then aggregate those needs to create standardized programmes and learning content. Often, this leads to a distortion of the actual learning needs and leaves employees wondering why they have been nominated to attend training that doesn't actually address their needs.

To create a collaborative learning environment it's necessary for organizations to embrace decentralization in their L&D strategy. It can be scary for L&D teams to relinquish total control over this process, but it doesn't have to be if they ease into it. The first step is to empower employees to create content internally that is designed to help employees accomplish their work more effectively. These resources do not need to be large courses at first, but can instead be smaller micro-lessons that can be completed at an employee's convenience. The important thing, however, is that this content is created internally and based on a process that identifies real learning needs within an organization, not just aggregated data based on individual training requests. This can help L&D teams build confidence in democratized learning and drum up the support from company leadership that is critical to maintaining an effective collaborative learning culture.

Step 2: Emphasize self-directed learning

At first glance, 'self-directed learning' might seem like an odd pillar of a learning system based around collaboration. After all, isn't the point of collaborative learning to work closely with other people? The confusion stems from what we mean when we talk about 'self-directed learning', which is emphatically *not* a solo activity.

In the context of collaborative learning, self-directed learning occurs when L&D teams meet employees where they are and help them do whatever it is they're trying to do. While self-directed learning has, in the past, been fruitfully used by L&D teams, the problem was that employees would engage with learning materials without being prompted. This meant it was divorced from the context where it could be most helpful. Instead, L&D teams can increase engagement and self-directed learning by using tools that identify the need for further development from an employee through performance feedback and then providing contextually relevant resources at the point of need. This will also foster employee autonomy and personal responsibility, which are key features of collaborative learning.

The popularity of self-directed learning is also backed up with data. In a recent survey about learning in the workplace, around three out of four learners said they wanted the freedom to take courses at their own pace and would take a course recommended by their manager.[9] Even more telling, when respondents were asked who should determine their learning needs, more than two-thirds chose 'myself' whereas the least chosen answer by far was 'executives'. These results underscore how important self-directed learning is to employees and the impact that leadership can have by transitioning to the role of a facilitator for self-directed learning.

Step 3: Promote knowledge sharing

An organization's greatest resource is its employees. This simple truth has been repeated so many times on motivational posters and in business seminars that it's almost become meaningless, a gesture at an ideal that is rarely exemplified in practice by management. But collaborative learning demands that this principle be fully embraced and put into action. The simple fact of the matter is that people learn from people. An organization's employees have the skills and subject-matter expertise to help it succeed and it is critical that organizations encourage their experts to share their knowledge with their peers.

'If only HP knew what HP knows,' Lew Platt, the former CEO of Hewlett-Packard, once lamented about his company's learning culture.[10] Platt's problem was that his company was segmented into informational silos that made it prohibitively difficult to share knowledge between departments. In this scenario, sales teams only learn about sales goals, marketing departments lack insight into product development, and no one has any idea what the engineers are tinkering with in the lab. When the left hand never knows what the right is doing, a company risks sleepwalking into an entirely preventable disaster. Just ask Platt, who recognized the company's informational silos were a problem only after it was too late to fix them. The result was HP's decades-long slide from a titan of Silicon Valley to what the *Wall Street Journal* recently described as a 'fading star of technology'.[11]

Sharing knowledge across an organization is about more than raw productivity, however. It also fosters transparency because employees are able to teach their peers about their work and gain visibility into other departments. This helps employees align on global strategy, promotes cross-team collaboration, and makes employees more invested in the company as a whole. Furthermore, knowledge sharing reduces the brain drain that occurs in top-down learning environments where institutional knowledge – the likes or dislikes of a client, the specifics of a technical process – is accumulated in individual employees. Those employees will take that knowledge with them when they leave unless their company has created systems to share knowledge so that crucial information can still be accessed even after an employee moves on.

Finally, promoting knowledge sharing within an organization encourages all employees to think like educators. This is critical because teaching others about a skill you know well is a great way to produce new insights that can lead to innovation. This is a well-known phenomenon in academia, where researchers regularly achieve 'eureka moments' during routine lectures to students, whose questions force them to think about the subject in a new light. When employees are involved in the course-creation process they must use decision-making and critical-thinking skills that can lead to similar breakthroughs. A team might not even realize the abundance of skills and knowledge possessed by its members unless they are encouraged to share it. In fact, a recent survey on workplace learning revealed that more than three out of four employees say that they have knowledge to share but have never been asked to. The companies that dare to ask the question will benefit from higher employee satisfaction, productivity and innovation.

Step 4: Choose the right learning tools

As with any major undertaking, it is important for organizations to choose the learning tools that will best support a collaborative learning environment. The key question that L&D teams need to ask when looking for the right platform to facilitate collaborative learning is simple: does this tool make it faster, easier and cheaper for employees to create content that meets their learning needs? In addition to features that make it simple for anyone to spin up a course or other resource, the learning software should also make it easy to update existing content and solicit feedback from learners. This ensures that the organization's learning content will always stay fresh because it provides a straightforward mechanism for learners to identify out-of-date information.

By abandoning one-size-fits-all solutions and embracing learning tools that are built to service a company's unique needs, its L&D team can focus on ensuring that its learning strategy delivers a return on investment for its organization. This is a substantial departure from the previous function of the L&D team, where a third of its working hours on average were spent building and sourcing learning content. As an organization's own experts assume this role in a collaborative learning environment, it creates the opportunity for L&D

professionals to become strategic partners and learning facilitators. This typically involves meeting with key stakeholders within the organization to understand their learning needs, facilitating the flow of learning content by helping any teams that may be struggling and strategizing about how to make learning even more effective for the organization's goals.

It's important for L&D teams to understand that collaborative learning technologies will never replace them. Instead, they are designed to unlock L&D superpowers by reducing the amount of administrative and low-value-add work in the company's learning processes. And since these technologies only augment the role of L&D professionals within an organization, that means they will be necessary but never sufficient for creating a collaborative learning environment. This was already recognized decades ago by the pioneers of collaborative learning when the sophisticated software we take for granted today was still a distant dream. 'Software structures can be constructed which will support group collaboration, however they can only facilitate the desired behaviour, not produce it,' one researcher observed in the 1990s. 'For the group to adapt a structure of interaction that is collaborative in nature, the instructor must mould, model, and encourage the desired behavior.'[12] This perfectly captures the future of the L&D profession as collaborative learning goes mainstream.

CASE STUDY

The power of community: How Busuu drives self-paced language learning through peer connections

As one of the world's biggest online language learning platforms, Busuu empowers people to learn new languages through a combination of self-paced study, live classes with dedicated expert tutors and access to a community of more than 120 million native speakers around the world. This mix of peer-driven learning is a great example of the power of the collective to create engaging learning experiences and help people upskill.

Busuu recognizes that social interaction drives every great learning experience, which is why it combines the convenience of self-paced study with peer interaction, helping learners connect with each other to offer help, guidance and encouragement. With a global community of learners, Busuu offers users the ability to increase their fluency in 14 different languages. And because learning through Busuu is so interactive, everyone who is a student on Busuu is also a teacher.

As a platform, Busuu encourages every language learner to actively engage with their community of fellow learners, offering tips and techniques to help each other develop. That's because Busuu has found that the users who engage the most with their peers through the platform are those who can improve their fluency faster, and with lasting results. By helping to correct and improve the exercises submitted by other learners, Busuu users are able to gain confidence in their own learning abilities, and feel more committed to their own learning as they see others progress.

This is a powerful example of the value of peer connection in learning. It's also a helpful illustration of learning across different formats, with the interplay between self-paced study, interaction with a community of other learners, and live expert lessons creating a virtuous circle of language development. This mix of learning modes gives Busuu users the ability to take what they've learned in their coursework and practised asynchronously in their community, and apply it directly in their live lessons.

With more and more businesses offering Busuu memberships to their teams, companies around the world are helping their employees develop their own language skills through making the right connections with a motivated peer group of other learners.

Notes

1   H Lee and C J Bonk. Collaborative learning in the workplace: Practical issues and concerns, *International Journal of Advanced Corporate Learning (iJAC)*, 2014, 7 (2), 10–17

2   J Peters and J Armstrong. Collaborative learning: People learning together to construct knowledge, *New Directions for Adult and Continuing Education*, 1998, 79, 75–85

3 P Dillenbourg, M Baker, A Blaye and C O'Malley (1996) The evolution of research on collaborative learning, in E Spada and P Reiman (eds) *Learning in Humans and Machine: Towards an interdisciplinary learning science*, Emerald Publishing

4 S Hiltz. Collaborative learning in asynchronous learning networks: Building learning communities, US Department of Education, 1998

5 R E Clark, D F Feldon, J J G van Merrienboer, et al. Cognitive task analysis, 14 October 2006, https://cdn-prod-pdfsimpli-wpcontent.azureedge.net/pdfseoforms/pdf-20180219t134432z-001/pdf/cognitive-task-analysis-pdf-format-free-download.pdf (archived at https://perma.cc/2WA9-NWFF)

6 D J Wood and B Gray. Toward a comprehensive theory of collaboration, *Journal of Applied Behavioral Science*, 1991, 27 (2), 139–62

7 P Drucker. Interview, *T&D Magazine*, 2000, 27

8 M Laal and S Ghodsi. Benefits of collaborative learning, *Procedia-Social and Behavioral Sciences*, 2012, 486–90

9 360Learning. What do your learners really want? nd, https://360learning.com/ebook/employee-engagement-survey/ (archived at https://perma.cc/8CQF-RK9L)

10 C G Sieloff. If only HP knew what HP knows: The roots of knowledge management at Hewlett-Packard, *Journal of Knowledge Management*, 1999, 3 (1), 47–53

11 C Lombardo. Xerox considers takeover offer for HP, *Wall Street Journal*, 6 November 2019, www.wsj.com/articles/xerox-considers-takeover-offer-for-hp-11573012201 (archived at https://perma.cc/7V67-UGBU)

12 S Hiltz. Collaborative learning in asynchronous learning networks: Building learning communities, US Department of Education, 1998

3

Why we need collaborative learning today

It may be true that the only constant in life is change, but these days the change seems to be happening faster than ever before. We live in an era of exponential growth in markets, users and technologies. The acceleration in all areas of the economy has created exceptional opportunities, but it has also created new demands on businesses in equal measure. Companies that are unable to stay nimble and adapt to the constant change are doomed to perish; those that implement the processes that foster organizational dynamism will thrive. L&D systems based on upskilling from within through collaborative learning are essential tools for future-proofing a business regardless of its industry. In this chapter we'll explore some of the dominant social and economic trends that are shaping the way organizations conduct their business, from training to retaining talent, and why collaborative learning is uniquely poised to deliver the results organizations need in an uncertain world.

The years have become days

When I sat down to write this book, the world was entering the second year of the Covid-19 pandemic. On this melancholy anniversary, I couldn't help but think of a quote attributed to Vladimir Lenin, the architect of the Soviet revolution, who remarked that 'there are decades when nothing happens; and there are weeks when decades happen'. It's hard to think of a more apt description of the unprecedented ways that the global pandemic has reshaped society.

Consider the mRNA coronavirus vaccines that pharmaceutical companies managed to produce at scale in only a matter of months in a heroic effort to limit the spread of the virus. The core technology – strands of messenger RNA that carry a genetic payload that teaches our bodies how to fend off an infection – has been under development for decades. But until the pandemic took the world by storm, mRNA vaccines were considered a curiosity with few prospects for meaningful applications. The researcher whose work laid the foundation for the coronavirus vaccines had received no accolades for her work and she toiled in relative obscurity for most of her career.[1] Now, the biotechnology she was instrumental in creating is being heralded as the future of preventative medicine.[2]

A remarkable feature of the global pandemic was how it dramatically accelerated latent trends in society. Some, like mRNA, were exotic. Others, like changes in the way we work, were more prosaic. Almost overnight, office buildings emptied out and makeshift workspaces were created in kitchens and spare bedrooms. The office happy hour took place via video call and many people seized the opportunity to move to a new town once physical proximity to their workplace was no longer a factor in their employment. At the same time, millions of workers used the abundance of downtime during the early days of the pandemic to reassess their career. Many of them decided that whatever they were doing when the world went into lockdown was no longer worth it and quit in such large numbers that we gave the phenomenon a name: the Great Resignation.

The seeds of these changes were planted long before the pandemic. For years, management professionals had been predicting the rise of remote work and the death of the office. While there was certainly a steady growth in the number of remote workers, surveys now suggest that only a third of workers want to return to the office full time.[3] A similar trend can be observed in employee job satisfaction. For the past decade, the percentage of American workers who consider themselves very satisfied with their job hovered at around 50 per cent.[4]

That leaves roughly 80 million workers wanting something better – it's no wonder they're quitting in droves.

There are no silver bullets in life. But when it comes to the challenges facing the modern organization, collaborative learning is a critical lifeline. By changing the way their organizations learn, L&D professionals can help their organization not only avoid hardship, but thrive. While this is hardly an exhaustive list, the biggest challenges facing companies in the coming years can be distilled into five broad categories: remote work, low engagement, employee burnout, media consumption and demographics.

Remote work

In 1997, Frances Cairncross, then the media editor of *The Economist*, made a bold prediction. The internet, she wrote, would cause jobs to flow out of cities and into rural areas. The new generation of telecommunications technologies heralded 'the death of distance' by enabling businesses and their employees to conduct their business wherever there happened to be a broadband connection.[5] Instead of our daily commute to the office, we would simply be able to take the on-ramp to the information superhighway. Remote work, once a luxury once reserved for jet-setting executives, was about to be democratized and accessible to knowledge workers everywhere.

In retrospect, Cairncross got it half right. Over the past two decades, the urbanization trend in countries around the world has actually accelerated, even as internet access became more ubiquitous. The outpouring of urbanites into the countryside never materialized, which speaks to the remarkable power of agglomeration effects – the economic efficiencies that come from co-location. Nevertheless, during that same period remote work dramatically increased. In 1997, the same year that Cairncross published her landmark book, only 7 per cent of employees worked at least one day of the week at home. By 2010, that number had increased to 9 per cent.[6] Over the past decade, however, something remarkable happened. By the end of 2019, around 20 per cent of workers in the US worked remotely at least one day a week. The global pandemic only accelerated this trend, and at the time I'm writing this more than half of American knowledge workers are remote. Many – perhaps most – have no intention of returning to the office.

The massive increase in fully remote and hybrid work arrangements over the past decade was largely a result of the rise of cloud-based SaaS (software as a service) products that enabled employees to work from anywhere.[7] Products like Zoom, Slack, Dropbox, Google Docs and others reduced the friction that was normally associated with moving office processes online. As remote work has become accessible to more people, the option to work from home at least part time has become table stakes during job negotiations. In fact, recent surveys suggest that nearly a quarter of American workers would take a 10–20 per cent pay cut in exchange for the ability to work remotely, and around half would quit their jobs if they were forced to come back into the office after going remote.[8] In addition, 38 per cent of working adults in the United Kingdom reported working remotely at least some of the time.[9] Clearly, remote work is a trend that isn't going away.[10] Indeed, some forecasts suggest that around half of all knowledge workers globally will be working remotely by the middle of this decade.[11]

Businesses that empower their employees to work remotely full time or part time enjoy many advantages.[12] They are able to hire more competitively and their workers are both happier and more productive. But at the same time remote work creates unique challenges, especially when it comes to creating an effective learning culture in an organization. In companies that employ hybrid or fully remote workers, onsite training becomes difficult to organize and employees can feel a sense of isolation or a lack of support in acquiring the skills they need to do their jobs.

Fortunately, many of the same technological solutions that enabled remote work can be harnessed by L&D teams to foster learning at a distance. Cloud-enabled collaborative learning platforms are built to allow employees to complete training and courses wherever they may be. While this is not unique to collaborative learning systems, their community-based design is a feature that isn't found on other learning platforms. The ability of employees to engage with their peers in learning exercises is the key to both effective learning and building a great culture in a hybrid or fully remote work environment. It destroys the sense of isolation many remote workers feel in their home office, facilitates the transfer of relevant knowledge to employees when they need it, and reverses another major challenge facing businesses today: low employee engagement.

CASE STUDY

How ShipHawk's 'flight school' drives great new hire onboarding by upskilling from within

ShipHawk is a leader in warehouse and fulfilment automation solutions, empowering customers to increase their fulfilment speed, accuracy and efficiency. To provide this high level of customer service, ShipHawk needs to support every one of its new hires to feel independent and confident in their roles from day one. They achieve this through the ShipHawk 'flight school': peer-driven learning experiences offering all the onboarding basics every new employee needs.

Today's supply-chain environment can be complex. That's why ShipHawk is so focused on helping companies manage their fulfilment costs by making sure that they're receiving products into the warehouse, picking orders efficiently, packaging in the smallest, most efficient package possible and also choosing the most cost-effective and customer-serving delivery method available. Given this highly technical area, it's crucial for ShipHawk's new hires to be able to benefit from the true depth of industry knowledge held by the company's subject-matter experts.

ShipHawk's 'flight school' for new hires offers exactly that. By partnering with ShipHawk's internal experts, the company's L&D leaders have built bespoke learning experiences offering an in-depth guide on how to manage shipping, picking, packing and warehousing within the supply-chain industry: how it's structured, how it operates from day to day and how it can be navigated. And given there is so much specialist terminology used in the shipping industry, ShipHawk's 'flight school' also includes dedicated primers on acronyms, insider slang and other niche language.

This 'flight school' helps give ShipHawk's new starters a solid foundation in company culture, industry trends and specialist product knowledge, leveraging peer expertise for the benefit of the collective. This attention to detail has paid dividends for ShipHawk so far, with new employees giving overwhelmingly positive feedback on the levels of collaboration and interactivity within the onboarding experience.

ShipHawk's 'flight school' perfectly showcases the benefits of collaborative learning. By leveraging internal experts to co-design their onboarding programme, the ShipHawk L&D team upskills new hires from within by giving them a tailored guide to the industry, the company and the product. This helps to maintain ShipHawk's competitive edge and ensure that every new hire can hit the ground running.

Low engagement

For years, low employee engagement has been a major concern for organizations. According to a Gallup survey of more than 110,000 business units across 54 industries, around two-thirds of US workers are considered 'not engaged' at work, of which about a quarter are *actively* disengaged, meaning they are not completing their work, they're hostile toward management, and/or they're looking for other jobs.[13] The low levels of employee engagement have held remarkably steady over the past two decades and have major consequences for organizations. Not only does having engaged employees improve a company's bottom line and its culture, it also makes the organization more resilient. But what exactly are we talking about when we talk about engagement? Answering this question is the first step toward making a positive change in an organization.

Employee engagement is a multifaceted metric, but it is typically defined as how committed an employee is to their organization or the degree of fulfilment they derive from their job. But these factors can be hard to quantify. As a result, a lot of business leaders tend to use an 'I know it when I see it' approach to keep a pulse on employee (dis)engagement in their organization. This works well enough for actively engaged or actively disengaged employees because they're easy to spot. If an employee is entrepreneurial and going above and beyond their job requirements, they're clearly engaged; if they're skipping work or spending most of their workday surfing the web, they're actively disengaged. But this heuristic doesn't really help us when it comes to those employees who are neither actively engaged nor actively disengaged, but merely not engaged. These employees do enough to get by and keep a low profile. This class represents a solid majority of US workers and figuring out how to engage them is critical to driving organizational success.

Study after study has found that engaged employees have a few key characteristics in common.[14] First, most of these employees tend to have a sense of purpose when it comes to their work. This could be contributing to the company's overall mission or the role they play within their team. They want to feel that their work matters and that their contribution makes a difference. Second, engaged employees feel supported by their peers and managers, who give the resources and feedback they need to do their jobs effectively. Third, engaged employees have a solid sense of their career trajectory. They feel that they are working toward something bigger and the work they accomplish moves them toward this goal. This is usually cultivated through clear communication about expectations and advancement opportunities from leadership.

But by far the biggest contribution to employee engagement is having opportunities for learning and development. Consider these stats: 80 per cent of workers say that learning a new skill at work would make them more engaged,[15] and 70 per cent of workers say they do not have the skills they need to become experts at their job.[16] In case it's not obvious, these are two sides of the same coin. Employees are hungry for knowledge and see skill development as one of the biggest motivators for showing up to work every day. This isn't the least bit surprising. As we'll see in the next chapter, humans are hardwired to learn and when we're cut off from the opportunity to develop our skills, we suffer both emotionally and cognitively. Yet when it comes to engaging this basic human need, companies have a lot of room for improvement.

The problem isn't that L&D is ignored by business leaders. Quite the opposite, in fact. A recent survey by LinkedIn found that 90 per cent of executives consider L&D a necessary benefit to their company.[17] But not all learning systems are created equal. It doesn't matter how much an executive cares about fostering engagement through skills development if they aren't using the right tools. This is why employee engagement rates have remained depressed for decades despite widespread support for robust L&D programmes in the business world. The majority of organizations are using learning platforms that are heralded by L&D and peripheral to employees. They don't meaningfully increase engagement and may result in employees checking out even more.

Collaborative learning tools have been shown to reliably increase employee engagement through L&D. The reason for this is that alternative learning systems treat L&D as just another to-do item on HR's checklist. But implementing collaborative learning involves a profound culture shift within an organization that fosters employee engagement along multiple dimensions at once.

First and foremost, it is the most effective way to transfer knowledge and new skills, which meets employees' needs for development. At the same time, it also endows employees with a sense of purpose by giving them greater visibility into the wider organization outside their own team and the pride that comes with working toward an ambitious goal alongside their peers. Moreover, collaborative learning also creates meaningful opportunities for career advancement by allowing employees to identify and cultivate the skills they need to progress. And, perhaps most importantly, collaborative learning creates a robust support network of peers and managers who help employees meet their learning goals. Together, these aspects of collaborative learning can push employee engagement to new heights and create long-lasting benefits that will sustain an organization.

Employee burnout

If you're anything like me, one of the most noticeable side effects of the Covid pandemic was a constant feeling of exhaustion. Part of this was undoubtedly a result of the general climate of fear and anxiety that came with this unprecedented health emergency. But there was also a general sense that I was working more than ever. Without the clear delineation between the office and home, it was difficult to put up boundaries to achieve any semblance of work–life balance. There was always time to answer one more email, make one more phone call, or review one more slide deck, and excuses were hard to come by. After all, it wasn't like I had dinner plans or concert tickets!

This feeling of exhaustion that so many of us experienced during the pandemic is a symptom of burnout. Although not a recognized medical condition, burnout is nonetheless very real.[18] It's a result of prolonged work-related stress and it can lead to feelings of detachment, cynicism, irritability and depression that make it hard to do much of anything at all. Widespread employee burnout predates the global pandemic and will be with us long after it's gone. Today, surveys suggest that roughly three-quarters of American workers have experienced burnout at their jobs and more than half of them have experienced burnout more than once.[19] Burnout is not just exclusive to America – finding ways to reduce employee stress is an urgent matter for business leaders everywhere and requires us to understand the root of the issue.

At this point, you may be shaking your head and thinking to yourself, ' Nick, it's so *obvious*: the reason employees are burned out is because they're given too much work!' I agree with you and so does the data.[20] But given that we are all on the same page about why employees are experiencing burnout, we need to ask ourselves why companies still insist on giving them even more work. Since the new millennium, the length of the average American's workday has increased by 1.4 hours and surveys show that nearly one in six Americans report working more than 60 hours a week.[21] These days, feeling stress in your job has, in the words of a recent *New Yorker* article on the subject, 'become a default metric for judging whether we are busy enough'.[22]

In short, burnout culture needs to change – and fast. The effects of employee burnout can be felt throughout an organization. It leads to lower productivity, lower customer satisfaction and lower employee retention. The challenge is addressing burnout without doing more damage in the process. A naive solution is to simply reduce the amount of work given to employees. But for many organizations – such as those working in critical industries like healthcare or aviation – there is no 'off' button. As a result, employers are getting creative with how they can reduce burnout by shifting the way the workload is distributed rather than eliminating it. A number of recent experiments with four-day work weeks, both at organizational and national levels, is an example of this in practice that shows a lot of promise.[23]

The learning culture of an organization has a big role to play in reducing employee burnout. Under current learning systems, many employees see courses as a burden that merely adds to their already substantial workload. This is an often overlooked result of relying on top-down learning systems where courses take months to produce and feel irrelevant by the time they make it in front of employees. At the same time, while digital learning platforms empower employees to take courses whenever and wherever they'd like, the fact of the matter is that the overwhelming majority of employees prefer to learn at work, including in the flow of work.[24] Since organizations typically don't reduce an employee's workload to make time for required training, each new course adds to employee stress. Furthermore, top-down approaches to L&D also tend to operate on strict timelines, despite most employees either preferring to learn at their own pace or at their point of need.

Collaborative learning can help organizations address this problem. Since collaborative learning is produced in a bottom-up fashion in response to employee needs, it's seen as a tool that helps them get their work done more effectively rather than an irrelevant burden that adds to their workload. It is, in a word, *personalized*. By empowering employees to learn what they need when they need it, organizations can eliminate one of the contributors to employee burnout. Rather than forcing every employee to take the same training regardless of whether it is relevant to their needs, which is sure to create stress and tension, collaborative learning ensures that employees engage with resources only when it can actually help them. And because collaborative learning is so effective at helping employees learn new skills, it can help reduce feelings of stress that are associated with real or perceived knowledge gaps. The key realization here is that 'burnout is about your workplace, not your people'.[25] Collaborative learning is a fundamentally different approach to an organization's L&D that simultaneously reduces employee stress while improving their productivity, but it is only effective if it is fully embraced at the organizational scale.

Media consumption

As one of the last generations to grow up in a world without the internet, I am at least a little envious of the quality and quantity of content that my children have access to. With virtually limitless mobile games, social platforms and shows streaming on demand, they may never know what it is like to experience true boredom – or even the frustration of finding nothing worthwhile to watch on television. They worship YouTube stars I've never even heard of, but I am assured that their reach and influence among preteens makes Lionel Messi seem like a nobody. For them, this is normal because they've never known any different. Yet I am constantly amazed at how fast our media habits have changed.

The rise of the social media platforms that have become hallmarks of Web 2.0 marked a watershed moment in the ways we produce and consume media. Now anyone with a smartphone and a computer can produce high-quality content for YouTube, Facebook, TikTok or Twitter and reach a global audience of millions. At the same time, we've become accustomed to a high degree of interactivity on these platforms. We can speak directly to our favourite content creators, crowd-source answers to our burning questions on Reddit or Stack Overflow, and totally customize our gaming experience on platforms like Roblox or Fortnite.

The new media regime is a marked departure from the unidirectional flow of media in the past. Whereas cable television or books were like a transmission from the creator to their audience, today's media is more like a conversation. It is fundamentally bidirectional and the line between the creator and audience is increasingly blurred. While YouTube or Reddit may seem like they have little to do with the L&D needs of a company, I believe that our shifting media consumption habits and organizational learning systems are deeply intertwined.

A useful analogy is to look at how the rise of consumer apps has led organizations to expect a more consumerized experience from their business-to-business (B2B) software. Now, the clunky on-premise solutions that dominated from the late 1980s to the early 2000s no longer cut it. Companies and their employees expect even the most mundane workflow software to have sleek interfaces, intuitive user experiences, around-the-clock support, and so on. The 'fun' personal apps we use in our day-to-day lives have raised our expectations for what we expect from the apps we use for business.

In much the same way, our shifting media consumption habits have also changed what we expect from a media experience in the workplace. We're no longer satisfied watching training content created by some production company that looks like it's 20 years old because it's still using Flash animation. Instead, employees want content created by their peers and they want it to be a social experience. They want to comment, like and share. They want to consume *and* create.

This is where collaborative learning platforms shine and why their time has come. They are a learning system built around the sensibilities of modern users. They enable anyone to become a content creator and respond to content through voting systems, comments and other modes of interaction. Not only does this dramatically increase engagement from users, it also fosters better learning outcomes. Bringing the social aspects of Web 2.0 into L&D software ensures it is always up to date because users can flag stale content. It creates opportunities for learners to encourage their peers and provide constructive feedback. And, most importantly, it ensures that content is always relevant because it is created by learners to address their own needs.

CASE STUDY
How Mitsubishi Electric used collaborative learning to train thousands of customer engineers

Mitsubishi Electric is a 100-year-old company that manufactures, installs and maintains a wide variety of electrical equipment for its customers, including hundreds of thousands of heat pumps and air conditioning units around the world. To make this happen, Mitsubishi Electric relies on an army of customer engineers who must be rigorously trained so they can make key decisions when they're out in the field helping customers.

When the Covid-19 pandemic hit, Mitsubishi Electric knew it had a problem. The company needed to train more than 2,500 customer engineers over the next year, but the shift to a remote work environment made it challenging or impossible to use its conventional training materials. Mitsubishi Electric needed a robust learning platform that efficiently scaled training programmes by capturing expert knowledge through courses made by its own employees. At the same time, the company needed a way to monitor the quality of the training materials and track course completions to ensure that its new customer engineers were meeting Mitsubishi Electric's standards. The company found its solution in 360Learning's collaborative tools.

By switching from a training paradigm that mostly involved trainers talking through a PowerPoint presentation in person to an online collaborative format, Mitsubishi Electric was able to scale its onboarding process like never before. Its old learning paradigm simply couldn't handle the large inflows of employees, but making training materials available digitally for new hires removed this limitation and allowed Mitsubishi Electric to scale its hiring initiatives as fast as possible. At the same time, it was able to dynamically respond to evolving customer and employee learning needs by launching webinars and other learning materials in a matter of days.

A bonus of Mitsubishi Electric's shift to collaborative learning was that it significantly boosted employee engagement by moving away from a 'Death by PowerPoint' approach to training. Instead of sitting through day-long training seminars, new employees could be trained on a flexible schedule, which meant they could spend more time interacting with customers while learning the nuts and bolts of their job. While Mitsubishi Electric didn't do away with its in-person seminars entirely, its shift to mostly online collaborative training allowed it to continuously iterate on content, analyse platform metrics to see what was working and then replicate the best training materials for in-person sessions.

In addition to overhauling its internal onboarding process, Mitsubishi Electric also leveraged collaborative learning tools to transform its customer training experience. Before adopting collaborative learning, the company had a year-long waiting list for customer training. By empowering employees to create customer training courses, Mitsubishi Electric was able to reduce the wait time to less than 30 days while achieving a 99 per cent customer training satisfaction rate.

Demographics

The global workforce is in the midst of a profound demographic shift that will have important repercussions for the way organizations learn over the next decade. The locus of this change is the Baby Boomers, which refers to workers born between 1946 and 1964. In the US, Boomers make up approximately one-fifth of the total population and were only recently surpassed by Millennials – those born between 1981 and 1996 – as the largest generation.[26] Although the last of the Baby Boomers will reach retirement age by the end of this decade, labour data shows that they are staying in the workforce longer. The US Bureau of Labor Statistics, for example, predicts that by 2029 more than 16 million Americans over the age of 65 will still be working. That means 1 out of every 10 workers in the US will be over the age of 65 by the end of the decade, which represents a staggering 55 per cent increase compared with the number of retirement-age workers in 2019.[27]

The ageing workforce will present unique challenges for businesses when it comes to implementing effective L&D programmes. The Boomers as well as their successors – Gen X – spent the majority of their careers in a pre-internet office environment. As such, they tend to be more reluctant to use new technologies in their day-to-day work compared with their younger peers who entered the workforce as digital natives. Although this trend is technology agnostic, it is starkest in the context of online learning.

In 2001, the US National Telecommunications and Information Administration (NTIA) began tracking participation in online classes by age group. At the time, an average of 4 per cent of internet users reported taking classes or training online. The low participation in e-learning was found across age groups, which makes sense given how new the technologies – and the internet itself – were at the time. But the most recent data released by the NTIA shows that over the past two decades a substantial variation between age groups has emerged when it comes to online learning. In 2019, more than 30 per cent of internet users between the ages of 15 and 24 reported taking an online class or training, compared with just 6 per cent of internet users over the age of 65.[28]

There are many reasons why older workers may participate less in online learning. It frequently can be attributed to a lack of confidence and proficiency with digital technologies. Other challenges arise from the general cognitive decline that happens with age, which makes it more difficult for older people to process information, ignore distractions like instant messages, or learn new technologies being deployed in their workplace. These aren't problems that can be ignored. Sometimes it is because organizations simply view training older workers as too expensive because they have far fewer working years left than their younger peers.[29] The majority of employees view on-the-job training as essential for career advancement and their employers see it as essential to ensuring that their business is competitive and productive. The risk is that older workers who don't participate in training that increasingly occurs in online environments will be pushed out of the labour force, but this is itself an untenable position. Older workers are essential to offset the shrinking pool of young workers. Not only are there far fewer workers in the prime of their career, but the data shows that their participation in the workforce is declining as well.[30] The urgent question for organizations going forward is how to design learning systems that will boost participation from older workers while transferring the skills they need to use modern digital tools.

Unsurprisingly, many HR professionals and management gurus say the solution is taking online learning technologies out of the equation. The logic is straightforward: if older workers already struggle using new technologies, using an e-learning system to teach them will only add to the confusion. I recently came across a representative sample of this line of thinking in an article written by a Canadian professor and published in the *Wall Street Journal*.[31] While this professor's diagnosis was correct – companies are not investing enough in training their older workers – his remedy was way off the mark. 'It is important to do that training right,' the professor wrote, 'And one crucial part of that is training older workers face to face and not online.'

The problem with this analysis is the same as with every critic of new technology who advocates going back to the way things were done before that technology burst onto the scene: it never happens. New technologies are like Pandora's Box. Once they've arrived, there's no going back to the way things were before. Plenty of dictators have tried to ban new technologies, but this almost always turns out to be a fool's errand. If the technology meaningfully improves our lives, we will always find a way to use it. This holds true for e-learning as well, which will only become more critical as remote work spreads and face-to-face training becomes impractical or impossible.

But we can forgive the professor's misguided conclusion because in one sense he is right. Most currently available learning systems *are* inadequate for training older workers. They are difficult to use and lack the support that he views as crucial to effectively train older workers. When compared to these systems, in-person learning may in fact be a superior option, especially if it is structured around peer-based support. 'In my research I found one type of training had a particularly big payoff: mentorship programmes that pair older workers with expert users,' the professor wrote. 'Instead of going to formal training sessions, older workers can call on these users at the precise moment they need help. This approach is also more informal and friendly, so that older workers feel more comfortable about seeking advice.'

One can only presume that this professor was entirely unfamiliar with collaborative learning because these features – peer support from experts, informal learning interactions, content built for the needs of individual learners, real-time feedback – are hallmarks of collaborative learning platforms. In fact, collaborative learning goes far beyond in-person training on all of these metrics because it replaces a one-to-one mentor relationship with a many-to-one mentor relationship. That means that older workers can always learn from the most knowledgeable expert across an entire organization, rather than relying on their assigned mentor in a department who may not be an expert in the area. Online collaborative learning systems are designed to create a robust peer-supported knowledge network that lowers the barriers to training faced by many older workers through intuitive interfaces. As organizations grapple with changing labour force demographics in the coming years, collaborative learning systems will be an essential tool for ensuring that all employees receive the training and learning resources they need to succeed.

Collaborative learning is what organizations need today

The five challenges described above are a few of the major headwinds that organizations can expect to face in the coming years. Effective learning and training programmes are critical for helping companies stay nimble and productive while addressing these challenges and helping employees advance their careers. Yet, as we've seen, not all learning systems are created equal. Collaborative learning is the most robust and effective system for creating and transferring knowledge within an organization, and it comes equipped with all the features that L&D teams need to future-proof their organization. While upskilling from within through collaborative learning is by no means a new pedagogical approach, the shifting demands of the business and needs of learners make it clear its time has come.

Notes

1 P Nair. QnAs with Katalin Karikó, *Proceedings of the National Academy of Sciences*, 2021, 118 (51), https://doi.org/10.1073/pnas.2119757118 (archived at https://perma.cc/76UZ-KEBT)
2 A Finley. The vast promise of mRNA technology, *Wall Street Journal*, 3 December 2021, www.wsj.com/articles/the-vast-promise-of-mrna-vaccines-covid-19-omicron-shots-pfizer-biontech-ms-cancer-11638554419 (archived at https://perma.cc/G236-HER9)

3   M Leonhardt. Over a third of workers want to return to the office full-time, *Fortune*, 30 August 2021, https://fortune.com/2021/08/30/hybrid-work-return-to-office-full-time-survey/?tpcc=nlceodaily (archived at https://perma.cc/CXZ5-9ZCX)

4   Pew Research Center. How Americans view their jobs, Pew Research Center's Social and Demographic Trends Project, 28 September 2021, www.pewresearch.org/social-trends/2016/10/06/3-how-americans-view-their-jobs/ (archived at https://perma.cc/FR5G-XENP)

5   F Cairncross (1997) *The Death of Distance*, Harvard Business School Press, Boston, MA

6   US Census Bureau. Home-based workers in the United States: 2010, Census.gov, 2021, www.census.gov/library/publications/2012/demo/p70-132.html (archived at https://perma.cc/Q9GJ-CXFQ)

7   Gartner. Gartner forecasts worldwide public cloud revenue to grow 17 per cent in 2020, Gartner, 2019, www.gartner.com/en/newsroom/press-releases/2019-11-13-gartner-forecasts-worldwide-public-cloud-revenue-to-grow-17-percent-in-2020 (archived at https://perma.cc/PGL2-VR99)

8   Pelta. Many workers have quit or plan to after employers revoke remote work, FlexJobs, 12 January 2022, www.flexjobs.com/blog/post/workers-quit-employers-revoke-remote-work (archived at https://perma.cc/F2RK-UQRL)

9   UK Office for National Statistics. Is hybrid working here to stay? 23 May 2022, www.gov.uk/government/statistics/is-hybrid-working-here-to-stay (archived at https://perma.cc/22MC-KGP8)

10 L Saad and B Wigert. Remote work persisting and trending permanent, Gallup, 31 October 2021, https://news.gallup.com/poll/355907/remote-work-persisting-trending-permanent.aspx (archived at https://perma.cc/2KRA-TAGD)

11 Gartner. Gartner forecasts 51 per cent of global knowledge workers will be remote by the end of 2021, Gartner, 2021, www.gartner.com/en/newsroom/press-releases/2021-06-22-gartner-forecasts-51-percent-of-global-knowledge-workers-will-be-remote-by-2021 (archived at https://perma.cc/28HR-8DUN)

12 GitLab. A complete guide to the benefits of an all-remote company, GitLab, nd, https://about.gitlab.com/company/culture/all-remote/benefits/ (archived at https://perma.cc/N7FZ-V5EZ)

13 J Harter. US employee engagement holds steady in first half of 2021, Gallup, 2021, www.gallup.com/workplace/352949/employee-engagement-holds-steady-first-half-2021.aspx (archived at https://perma.cc/Q29L-DX48)

14 Gallup. What is employee engagement and how do you improve it? Gallup, nd, www.gallup.com/workplace/285674/improve-employee-engagement-workplace.aspx (archived at https://perma.cc/B75J-A8UA)

15 Udemy. Udemy workplace boredom study, Udemy, 2016, https://info.udemy.com/rs/273-CKQ-053/images/2016_Udemy_Workplace_Boredom_Study.pdf (archived at https://perma.cc/9D92-DWV2)

16 Gartner. Setting L&D leaders up for success: Human resources, Gartner, nd, www.gartner.com/en/human-resources/role/learning-development (archived at https://perma.cc/XY4W-4XC7)

17 HemsleyFraser. 90% of businesses say agile learning cultures are 'important' or 'extremely important', HemsleyFraser, 13 April 2022, www.hemsleyfraser.com/en-gb/insights/90-businesses-say-agile-learning-cultures-are-important-or-extremely-important (archived at https://perma.cc/2R5X-QU2P)

18 World Health Organization. Burn-out an 'occupational phenomenon': International Classification of Diseases, World Health Organization, 2019, www.who.int/news/item/28-05-2019-burn-out-an-occupational-phenomenon-international-classification-of-diseases (archived at https://perma.cc/EN2Q-FHRQ)

19 Deloitte United States. Workplace burnout survey, Deloitte United States, 2020, www2.deloitte.com/us/en/pages/about-deloitte/articles/burnout-survey.html (archived at https://perma.cc/SKP6-H3JD)

20 B Wigert and S Agrawal. Employee burnout, Part 1: The 5 main causes, Gallup, 2018, www.gallup.com/workplace/237059/employee-burnout-part-main-causes.aspx (archived at https://perma.cc/R5BR-NP39)

21 T-P Chen and R A Smith. American workers are burned out, and bosses are struggling to respond, *Wall Street Journal*, 2021, www.wsj.com/articles/worker-burnout-resignations-pandemic-stress--11640099198 (archived at https://perma.cc/M5CY-AT8F)

22 C Newport. Why do we work too much? *New Yorker*, 30 August 2021, www.newyorker.com/culture/office-space/why-do-we-work-too-much (archived at https://perma.cc/NND7-34PG)

23 BBC News. Four-day week 'an overwhelming success' in Iceland, BBC, 6 July 2021, www.bbc.com/news/business-57724779 (archived at https://perma.cc/L4JC-Z2LM)

24 LinkedIn. 2018 workplace learning report, LinkedIn, 2018, https://learning.linkedin.com/content/dam/me/learning/en-us/pdfs/linkedin-learning-workplace-learning-report-2018.pdf (archived at https://perma.cc/HC68-H5GZ)

25 J Moss. Burnout is about your workplace, not your people, *Harvard Business Review*, 2019, https://hbr.org/2019/12/burnout-is-about-your-workplace-not-your-people (archived at https://perma.cc/5BC5-NXBW)

26 R Fry. Millennials overtake Baby Boomers as America's largest generation, Pew Research Center, 2020, www.pewresearch.org/fact-tank/2020/04/28/millennials-overtake-baby-boomers-as-americas-largest-generation (archived at https://perma.cc/W5VU-2DAL)

27 NCCI. Latest trends in worker demographics, NCCI, www.ncci.com/Articles/Documents/Insights-LatestTrendsWorkerDemo.pdf (archived at https://perma.cc/ZBV4-JZVW)

28 R Goldberg. Nearly a third of American employees worked remotely in 2019, NTIA Data Show, National Telecommunications and Information Administration, US Department of Commerce, 2020, www.ntia.gov/blog/2020/nearly-third-american-employees-worked-remotely-2019-ntia-data-show (archived at https://perma.cc/7U7F-8DYM)

29 I Hecker, S Spaulding and D Kuehn. Digital skills and older workers, Urban Institute, 2021, www.urban.org/sites/default/files/publication/104771/digital-skills-and-older-workers_0.pdf (archived at https://perma.cc/KV3C-T8HH)

30 US Bureau of Labor Statistics. Down and down we go: The falling US labor force participation rate, *Monthly Labor Review*, US Bureau of Labor Statistics, 2018, www.bls.gov/opub/mlr/2018/beyond-bls/down-and-down-we-go-the-falling-us-labor-force-participation-rate.htm (archived at https://perma.cc/X7R9-J5L6)

31 S Tams. How to help older workers learn new technology, *Wall Street Journal*, 28 November 2021, www.wsj.com/articles/how-to-help-learn-old-employees-learn-new-technology-11637608125 (archived at https://perma.cc/5E6W-BGEY)

4

The science of shared expertise

In the early 1990s, a group of neurophysiologists at the University of Parma in northern Italy made an amazing discovery. For years, the researchers had been observing the brain activity in macaques, a type of small brown monkey found throughout much of the world that is frequently used as a model for neurobiological research because its brain architecture is very similar to our own.[1] The Italian scientists had set out to study the brain cells – known as neurons – responsible for controlling hand movements, which they would monitor using electrodes attached to the monkey's head as it reached for pieces of food.

The team's experiments were pretty standard neuroscience fare, but they led to an insight that has tantalized brain researchers ever since. In 1992, the Italians reported that the neurons that were activated when a monkey reached for a piece of food were also activated when that monkey watched another monkey reach for food.[2] Only a few years later, these so-called 'mirror neurons' were discovered to be present in the human brain, too. Originally, mirror neurons were thought to be concentrated in the brain regions responsible for language and motor coordination, but they have since been shown to be present in several areas of the brain, including those responsible for memory and sensory perception.[3]

Thirty years after they were discovered, the jury is still out on the exact function of mirror neurons.[4] They may help us understand others' intentions, foster empathy and acquire language. But what unites all the possible functions of mirror neurons is learning, whether that's a motor skill or a language.[5] The existence of mirror neurons is some of the strongest biological evidence that humans are hardwired to learn by watching others. This is most obvious in the case of infants and young children, who learn new skills by explicitly imitating their parents and peers. And, as you might expect, neuroresearch has shown that mirror neurons already develop in infants during their first year of life.[6]

Of course, it's not just newborns who learn this way; adults do, too. Observational learning driven by mirror neurons comes to us naturally, but there are ways to deliberately elevate this learning style to make it even more effective. Collaborative learning pairs our natural proclivity to learn from others with active learning, a pedagogical approach where learners are actively involved in knowledge creation through group interactions and applied thinking. Active learning has been proven to increase engagement, critical thinking, comprehension and knowledge retention, but most learning platforms still rely on passive instructional methods such as traditional lectures where information flows in one direction: from the teacher to the student. Like observational learning, the effectiveness of active learning is rooted in neuroscience. We ignore or suppress our natural instincts to learn from others and actively participate in knowledge creation at our peril.

Over the past few chapters we've seen how upskilling from within through collaborative learning can be used to enhance an organization's learning practices, boost employee engagement and help businesses navigate some of today's biggest challenges. If you're feeling a bit sceptical, I can't say I blame you. Collaborative learning really does sound too good to be true. But this approach to knowledge creation isn't snake oil, it's science. As we'll see throughout this chapter, the reason collaborative learning is so effective is because it is modelled around the way humans *actually* learn – through peer observation and active participation – instead of how we generally *imagine* they learn. Collaborative learning works because it harnesses both fundamental neurobiology and the higher-level processes of cognitive psychology. Its potency as a learning paradigm doesn't require a blind leap of faith. All you need to do is follow the data.

Back to the future with active learning

Active learning is not a new concept. The idea of placing students at the centre of the learning experience instead of the teacher has been around for at least a century. But advocates of this pedagogical approach mostly relied on anecdotal evidence to support their claims of the effectiveness of active learning.[7] It wasn't until relatively recently that scientific data began to emerge that demonstrated the incredible benefits of active learning beyond a shadow of a doubt. Although most active learning research has occurred in the context of secondary and post-secondary schools, the lessons from this research are directly applicable to implementing collaborative learning in non-educational organizations.

Scientific research on active learning really began to hit its stride in the early 1990s. Over the course of the preceding decade, researchers were increasingly sounding the alarm about the state of higher education. In particular, educators flagged noticeable gaps between teaching and learning, teaching and testing, and educational research in practice.[8] In other words, passive approaches to knowledge creation such as the university lecture didn't translate into improved outcomes for students as measured by either knowledge retention or test performance, yet educators remained stuck in the old ways of teaching despite an abundance of evidence that active learning methods improved outcomes for students. When researchers probed why this was the case, they found that more often than not it was a matter of professors who were reluctant to step outside their comfort zone by transitioning away from passive lecture-driven teaching formats, and those who were willing to implement active learning strategies often lacked the information or institutional support they needed to make the change.

In response to these challenges, the Association for the Study of Higher Education and the Educational Resources Information Center at George Washington University published a landmark report of the state of active learning in higher education in 1991.[9] The goal of the report was to provide a comprehensive overview of different strategies for fostering active learning in higher education that used 'research-based rather than descriptive studies'. Although it wasn't exactly a how-to book, the report identified ways that educators could modify lectures to more actively involve students, launch more stimulating discussions among learners and overcome common barriers to implementing active learning techniques in a classroom. Importantly, the conclusions outlined in the report were backed by data. Given how tricky it can be to pin down exactly what constitutes active learning, the researchers prioritized active learning strategies that were backed by data showing they resulted in statistically significant improved outcomes for learners compared with passive strategies.

The ASHE-ERIC report on active learning marked a turning point for the field. Over the next decade, educational researchers quantified the effects of active teaching methods in primary, secondary and post-secondary schools. And the more data they collected, the more evidence they found of active learning's effectiveness in creating and transmitting knowledge. In 1998 this flurry of research on active learning culminated in a massive study comparing the outcomes of active and passive learning strategies that remains one of the largest comparative studies in the field to this day.[10]

The study was led by Richard Hake, a professor at Indiana University who had spent most of his career as a 'hard-core condensed-matter-physics researcher' before transitioning to studying the way that physics is taught to students.[11] Hake examined the test scores of more than 6,500 undergraduate physics students across 62 introductory courses and divided them into groups based on whether they had received active or passive instruction from their teachers. His results were staggering. Hake found that students enrolled in the active learning courses had average performance gains that were nearly twice as high as those in passive learning settings. Moreover, Hake found that students who were engaged with active learning strategies had enhanced problem-solving abilities as measured by a common test.[12]

The evidence pointing to improved outcomes for learners has continued to pile up over the two decades since Hake's study. In 2014, a group of researchers at the University of Washington compared active and passive strategies on learning outcomes and once again found that active learning dramatically improves exam performance compared with traditional methods. But they went a step further. Not only does active learning improve outcomes, passive learning actually seems to make students more likely to perform *worse*. The researchers found that students in passive settings were around 1.5 times more likely to fail compared with students in active learning environments. In fact, the differences in outcomes between the two groups were so stark that the researchers speculated that 'if the experiments analysed here had been conducted as randomized controlled trials of medical interventions, they may have been stopped for benefit – meaning that enrolling patients in the control condition might be discontinued because the treatment being tested was clearly more beneficial'.[13]

In any case, by the turn of the millennium, the growing piles of data had already made it impossible to deny the advantages of active learning. In 2001, Lori Breslow, the founding director of the Teaching & Learning Laboratory at MIT, summarized her perspective of educators' attempts to implement active learning in the post-secondary classrooms in bold terms. 'One finding, in particular, is so consistent that it should be singled out for special attention,' Breslow wrote in an internal MIT newsletter for her colleagues. 'Put simply, it is this: Researchers have seen that when students themselves are actively involved in the learning process, their learning improves. This finding, far from being an abstraction of interest only to a small group of academicians in the field, has direct consequences for what we do in the classroom.'[14]

What active learning does to our brains

At the time that university educators were quantifying the effects of active learning on student outcomes, neuroscientists already understood that 'learning changes the physical structure of the brain'.[15] When we encounter new information it forges new connections between the neurons in our brain and these connections represent new knowledge. If we are repetitively exposed to the same information, the connections that represent that information grow stronger and we would say that we are learning. Conversely, if we are only infrequently exposed to a piece of information, the neural connections will grow weak and we will have effectively 'forgotten' that knowledge. The question facing learning scientists is how active learning seemed to forge these neural connections so much more effectively than passive learning strategies.

To understand how active learning changes our brain, researchers need a way to study our brain as it learns. Although neuroimaging techniques date back to the 1970s, neuroscientists added a powerful new tool to their repertoire in the 1990s with the advent of functional magnetic resonance imaging (fMRI). This neuroimaging technique reveals changes in blood flow throughout the brain, which can be mapped to neural activity because more blood flows to areas of the brain that are being used.

What neuroscientists found when they peered into the brains of active learners with fMRI is that this learning style activated far more areas of the brain at once than conventional passive learning. This makes sense – when active learning occurs, the brains of students must engage in multiple sensory, cognitive, emotional and social processes all at once. These processes may be rooted in very different areas of the brain, which requires forging many new connections between those areas. And that requires the hippocampus, the part of the brain that is deeply implicated in memory formation and as such is almost always involved with learning.

The hippocampus can create connections with various regions throughout the cortex, the outer layer of the brain associated with high-level processes like emotion, reasoning or language. When a student is engaged in active learning, it likely involves processes that are handled by the cortex. It may have an emotional component because the learner is working with peers who they consider friends, a logical component because the learner must reason through a problem, and a linguistic component because the learner may have to articulate their thoughts in writing or to their peers. As a result, many different areas of the brain will be firing at once in an active learning scenario and the hippocampus plays the role of a matchmaker by forging connections between these active regions of the brain. As the active learning continues, those connections between the cortical regions grow stronger.[16]

At the neurobiological level, this is why active strategies produce better outcomes for learners. Whereas passive learners may create strong neural connections in only one area of the brain, active learners create strong neural connections across many regions of their brain. This improves the likelihood that the knowledge stored in those neural connections will persist as memories that the learner can retrieve in the future. Indeed, the neural connections created through active learning have proven to be extremely durable.

One of the most potent examples of this comes from the Abecedarian Project, a longitudinal study that began in 1971 following a group of dozens of people for five decades to understand how exposure to enhanced learning techniques in early childhood shaped brain development over the course of their lifespan. Beginning at between 3 and 21 weeks of age, a group of children began receiving specialized education support built around active learning techniques five days a week, 50 weeks a year, for five straight years.[17] When researchers later scanned the brains of these individuals when they were around 40 years old, they found that the children who had been raised on active learning had larger brains overall than the study's control group, as well as larger individual brain regions associated with facilities like cognitive control. 'To our knowledge, this is the first experimental evidence on a link between known early educational experiences and long term changes in humans,' one of the study's authors wrote.[18]

The role of experts in active learning

So if we know that active learning can have profoundly positive effects on the structure of the brain, a pressing question is how to create learning environments that foster these changes. More to the point, it is imperative that we understand how the role of the teacher changes in active learning contexts, which is one of the primary points of differentiation between passive learning settings. According to MIT's Breslow, in active learning scenarios, 'teachers are not seen as fonts of information, but function more as mentors or coaches'. This doesn't mean that the knowledge of a teacher is irrelevant, it just changes the way the teacher conveys that information.

An analogy from professional sports is useful here. The coach of a football team has a lot of knowledge that the players need to operate at the highest level – a playbook crafted from years of experience, intelligence about a competitor, and so on – but the coach can't simply tell their players this information and expect them to win. They need to get out on the pitch to practise with their teammates and the coach can use their expert knowledge to ensure the players are practising effectively and advancing toward the shared goal of winning the match.

This is not an idle analogy. The idea that people learn best when they're able to engage with a teacher or subject-matter expert acting as a guide is also backed by science. Consider an experiment run by Antonio Battro, an Argentinian professor of neurocognition and education who is renowned as a leading expert on the ways that education shapes our brains. In 2013 Battro led a team of researchers in an experiment that sought to understand how dynamics between students and a teacher or subject-matter expert influenced learning.[19] The experiment involved 17 student–expert pairs reading a dialogue that required the expert to ask the learner questions and vice versa. During these dialogues, the researchers measured the brain activity of both the teacher and the learner using near-infrared spectroscopy, which uses light absorption in red blood cells to measure oxygen levels in the brain as a proxy for brain activity.

What Battro and his colleagues found was that when the learner and the expert asked questions of each other, the levels of brain activity increased in both people. When no questions were asked, the brain activity of the student and teacher also fell in tandem. The importance of this result for the structure of active learning environments can't be overstated. It is critical that active learning makes room for robust interactions between a subject-matter expert and a pupil in order to engage both parties in the learning process.[20] Not only will this lead to better knowledge retention for the learner, it can also increase the quality of the learning material itself.[21] Experts contribute their most valuable knowledge when they are motivated to do so based on their engagement with other people. At the same time, it also allows teachers and subject-matter experts to progressively improve their course through active and iterative feedback from their students. This is the science behind using internal expertise to upskill from within, creating more enriching and engaging experiences for both experts and learners.

The active learning paradox

The data pointing to the superiority of active learning compared with passive learning has been mounting for decades. But this forces us to face an uncomfortable question: if active learning is so great, why aren't more people using its techniques in learning contexts? As one group of educational researchers noted in 2021, 'the adoption of active learning has been slow'.[22] The curious gap between experts who realize the benefits of active learning and those who actually implement it in classrooms has been a preoccupation of learning scientists for years and they have produced a spate of research unpacking why this might be the case and what can be done about it.

At least part of the reason why active learning isn't being widely adopted is that people aren't particularly good at judging whether they are actually learning. In 2019, a team of Harvard researchers working in various STEM departments ran a study to compare the perceptions of students engaged in active or passive classrooms about their educational progress with their actual learning as measured by a test of the material covered in those classrooms.[23] The results were surprising. Students in active learning classrooms routinely reported that they felt like they weren't learning as much as they were in a passive learning environment characterized by a teacher lecturing their students. Yet when it came time to take a test on what they had learned, the students who had received the material in an active setting performed far better than those in the passive setting. In other words, although the active learners *felt* like they were learning less, they were actually learning far more.

'Deep learning is hard work,' the lead author of the study told journalists when asked for an explanation of this paradox. 'The effort involved in active learning can be misinterpreted as a sign of poor learning. On the other hand, a superstar lecturer can explain things in such a way as to make students feel like they are learning more than they actually are.'[24]

But inaccurate perceptions about active learning are only part of the problem. A staggering number of reports show that both teachers and students often resist the idea of moving from a passive learning style to an active one despite the likelihood of improving learning outcomes. From the teachers' perspective, the barriers to active learning typically concentrate around concerns about their effectiveness and concerns about the amount of time required for active learning (both for preparation and during instruction).[25] As we saw above, there is little reason for concerns about the effectiveness of active learning, and there is a wealth of research showing that active learning strategies need not be more time intensive for educators than passive approaches.[26]

What is less clear is how to overcome student resistance to active learning methods. It's not even clear whether learners *are* more resistant to active learning strategies or if this is just a baseless fear of educators. There is plenty of evidence showing that learners have positive,[27] mixed[28] or negative[29] responses to active learning techniques. For now, science can't definitively say whether students actually prefer active learning, but it has shown us that active learning improves learner outcomes and why it is so effective at a biological level. To the extent that learners do resist active learning techniques, successfully implementing these strategies in an organization mostly becomes an exercise in culture building and fostering employee behaviours that lend themselves to better learning outcomes across the organization.

Indeed, whether or not a learner prefers active learning is almost beside the point. It's kind of like eating vegetables. Plenty of people profess not to like them – or certainly don't *prefer* them – but they're indisputably good for you and it can cause serious health issues if they're entirely removed from your diet. The question is how to get someone who doesn't like vegetables to eat them anyway. Perhaps the best way is to enhance their flavour. If the only vegetable dish someone has ever known was steamed brussels sprouts, it's no wonder why they might be resistant to more veggies on their plate. But sear those brussels sprouts in a pan and toss them with some choice herbs and you've created a whole new dining experience. Better yet, introduce them to an entirely different vegetable and flavour profile to demonstrate that veggies don't always have to be bland and tasteless.

The same is true for the active learning techniques employed in collaborative learning. Learners may be resistant to these techniques at first because all they've ever known is passive, top-down learning environments. Indeed, research shows that many learners *prefer* passive learning techniques and tend to overestimate their effectiveness.[30] But if new approaches to knowledge creation and transmission are introduced throughout an organization in an engaging way that addresses the learner's specific needs, they will win over even the most diehard sceptics. In Chapter 8 we'll explore some of the common obstacles faced by organizations implementing collaborative learning and strategies for addressing these challenges in more detail.

Observational learning + active learning = collaborative learning

For most of this chapter, we've looked at the science of the two main elements of collaborative learning – observational and active learning – in the context of explicitly educational organizations like primary schools and universities. This is a side effect of the vast majority of research on different pedagogical approaches being rooted in school settings, but a growing body of evidence shows that the insights about collaborative learning that are gleaned in the classroom can be readily applied in situations or organizations where education is not a primary function.[31]

Properly speaking, collaborative learning is a subset of active learning.[32] Whereas there are many different active learning processes, such as think–pair–share or minute papers, that can be combined in various ways to achieve a learning objective,[33] the techniques that constitute collaborative learning are more circumscribed and stable over time. For example, collaborative learning draws from our innate tendencies to learn from others through its emphasis on peer feedback and leveraging experts within an organization. At the same time, collaborative learning takes a page from active learning by centring learners and letting them both express their learning needs and create their own solutions to address those needs.

By narrowing the purview of active learning to explicitly address those situations defined by learner-led interactions, collaborative learning also lends itself particularly well to the needs of organizations. Whereas active learning techniques writ large may work well for classrooms, organizations tend to be much more dynamic and thus require more stable patterns for knowledge creation and transmission. Collaborative learning effectively implements guide rails to help learners achieve their goals without being overly prescriptive. As a result, the limitations that collaborative learning places on active learning techniques don't reduce its effectiveness. Rather, by selectively applying elements of observational and active learning techniques in an explicitly learner-driven environment, collaborative learning is able to enhance the ability for organizations to meet their learning goals. Simply put, upskilling from within through collaborative learning is greater than the sum of its parts.[34]

In earlier chapters, we've already seen how collaborative learning can be used effectively in growth-stage organizations, as well as established titans of industry like Mitsubishi Electric and McDonald's. These case studies were descriptive, but given the theme of this chapter I'd like to end with a short description of two of the most exciting experiments in educational research that demonstrate the profound power of collaborative learning with real-world data.

CASE STUDY

Sugata Mitra's 'Hole in the Wall'

Both experiments were run by Sugata Mitra, an Indian computer scientist widely regarded as the leader of educational research in the 21st century. In 1999,

Mitra left an internet-connected computer in a New Delhi slum. Most of the residents of the slum had never even seen a computer, much less used one. The computer proved to be a hit among children in the slum, who quickly learned how to use the device to record themselves singing, send emails and play games online. This was remarkable due to both their unfamiliarity with computers and the fact that they were programmed in English, a language none of the children spoke. For Mitra, the lessons from this experiment were twofold. First, people have a remarkable capacity to direct their own learning with minimal intervention from an outside expert. Second, learning is most effective when the content is fun and engages learners as a group.

Mitra replicated his 'hole-in-the-wall' experiment in rural villages around the world with similarly successful results.[35] But he wasn't finished. In a follow-on experiment to probe the limits of self-education, Mitra left a computer in a Tamil-speaking village in southern India that was loaded with information on biotechnology written in English. He told the children in the village that there was some really difficult information on this computer and that he wouldn't be surprised if they didn't understand a word of it. Before he left, he gave the students an exam on the information contained in the computer. Unsurprisingly, all the children in the village completely failed.

But when Mitra returned to the village two months later and re-tested the children, he found their scores had improved significantly – in some cases rising to as high as 30 per cent. The students had not only taught themselves how to use a computer to access information written in another language, they had actually managed to internalize that information, too. Mitra found that the students had taught themselves about complex subjects like DNA replication and genetic disease, but even more importantly he found that some of the children had taken on the role of an instructor and helped the others learn the material. For Mitra, this was clear evidence that peer collaboration and peer-led instruction could produce superior learning outcomes compared with conventional techniques.

Years later, Mitra launched a new study to delve deeper into the role that peer support plays in the learning process. Known as the Granny Cloud experiment, Mitra again tasked a group of students to teach themselves concepts in biotechnology despite having no previous background in the subject. But as the students learned this subject, he encouraged their peers to play the role of a grandmother and to stand behind them and offer words of encouragement as they studied. Two months later, Mitra gave these students an exam on the material and found that their scores were comparable to students who had studied the material with a trained teacher at a school in Delhi.

The remarkable success of the Granny Cloud experiment impressed upon Mitra the fundamental importance of positive reinforcement and peer feedback in the learning process. In fact, the results were so overwhelmingly positive that Mitra later created a school where grandmothers in the United Kingdom would volunteer one hour a week to participate in an online course with students in rural areas of the country. None of the grandmothers who participated in the online school had a background in the subjects the students were studying, but their encouragement and ability to stimulate conversation nevertheless improved student outcomes.[36]

Mitra's pioneering experiments show the remarkable effects of collaborative learning in action. While a slum in Delhi or a grandmother in the UK may seem to have little relevance to the learning needs of a business, these examples all serve to highlight why collaborative learning is so effective regardless of the context in which it is used. Time and time again, science has shown us that upskilling from within through collaborative learning can achieve amazing outcomes by leveraging the power of emotional support, learner-directed education, constructive feedback and engaging content in an environment that fosters peer interaction.

Notes

1   D T Gray and C A Barnes. Experiments in macaque monkeys provide critical insights into age-associated changes in cognitive and sensory function, *Proceedings of the National Academy of Sciences*, December 2019, 116 (52), 26247–54, www.pnas.org/content/116/52/26247 (archived at https://perma.cc/G9S3-PRJQ)

2   G di Pellegrino, L Fadiga, L Fogassi, et al. Understanding motor events: A neurophysiological study, *Experimental Brain Research*, 1992, 91, 176–80, https://link.springer.com/article/10.1007/BF00230027 (archived at https://perma.cc/36LN-RR4R)

3   T Ehrenfeld. Reflections on mirror neurons, *Association for Psychological Science*, 2011, www.psychologicalscience.org/observer/reflections-on-mirror-neurons (archived at https://perma.cc/4FRY-5FMF); J M Kilner and R N Lemon. What we know currently about mirror neurons, *Current Biology*,

2 December 2013, www.ncbi.nlm.nih.gov/pmc/articles/PMC3898692 (archived at https://perma.cc/M8TT-63MH)

4   J M Taylor. Mirror neurons after a quarter century: New light, new cracks, Science in the News, Harvard University, 2016, https://sitn.hms.harvard.edu/flash/2016/mirror-neurons-quarter-century-new-light-new-cracks/ (archived at https://perma.cc/CC2T-YFPG)

5   R Ramsey, D Kaplan and E Cross. Watch and learn: The cognitive neuroscience of learning from others' actions, *Trends in Neurosciences*, 2021, 44 (6), 478–91, https://doi.org/10.1016/j.tins.2021.01.007 (archived at https://perma.cc/H79C-22T3)

6   T Falck-Ytter, G Gredeback and C van Hofsten. Infants predict other people's action goals, *Nature Neuroscience*, 2006, 9 (7), 878–79, https://doi.org/10.1038/nn1729 (archived at https://perma.cc/6LG5-UTW7)

7   G H Mead (1934) *Mind, Self and Society*, University of Chicago Press, Chicago

8   P Cross. In search of zippers, *American Association for Higher Education Bulletin*, 31 May 1988, https://eric.ed.gov/?id=ED299895 (archived at https://perma.cc/68CC-5WMC)

9   C C Bonwell and J A Eison. Active learning: Creating excitement in the classroom: 1991 ASHE-ERIC Higher Education Reports, ERIC Clearinghouse on Higher Education, 30 November 1990, https://eric.ed.gov/?id=ED336049 (archived at https://perma.cc/NL7D-LFVH)

10   University at Buffalo. Evidence of active learning's effectiveness, University at Buffalo, 2019, www.buffalo.edu/catt/develop/design/designing-activities/active-learning-effectiveness.html (archived at https://perma.cc/5TEV-GZTS)

11   R Hake. Research in physics education, Indiana University, https://web.physics.indiana.edu/hake/ (archived at https://perma.cc/LTL9-C4UD)

12   R Hake. Interactive-engagement versus traditional methods: A six-thousand-student survey of mechanics test data for introductory physics courses, *American Journal of Physics*, 1998, 66 (1), 64–74, https://doi.org/10.1119/1.18809 (archived at https://perma.cc/S6A6-36VP)

13   S Freeman, S L Eddy, M McDonough and M P Wenderoth. Active learning increases student performance in science, engineering, and mathematics, *Proceedings of the National Academy of Sciences*, 2014, 111 (23), 8410–15, https://doi.org/10.1073/pnas.1319030111 (archived at https://perma.cc/LB9B-ALXG)

14   L Breslow. New research points to the importance of using active learning in the classroom, Teach Talk, MIT, http://web.mit.edu/fnl/vol/121/breslow9.htm (archived at https://perma.cc/MKE9-L68U)

15   National Research Council (1999) *How People Learn: Brain, mind, experience, and school*, National Academies Press, Washington, DC

16 C Hoogendoorn. The neuroscience of active learning, City Tech, 15 October 2015, https://openlab.citytech.cuny.edu/writingacrossthecurriculum/2015/10/15/the-neuroscience-of-active-learning/ (archived at https://perma.cc/4Y5K-9ET7)

17 M J Farah, S Sternberg, T A Nichols, et al. Randomized manipulation of early cognitive experience impacts adult brain structure, *Journal of Cognitive Neuroscience*, 2021, 33 (6), 1197–209, https://doi.org/10.1162/jocn_a_01709 (archived at https://perma.cc/VU73-BSUD)

18 M J Farah, S Sternberg, T A Nichols, et al. Randomized manipulation of early cognitive experience impacts adult brain structure, *Journal of Cognitive Neuroscience*, 2021, 33 (6), 1197–209, https://doi.org/10.1162/jocn_a_01709 (archived at https://perma.cc/VU73-BSUD)

19 A M Battro, C I Calero, A P Goldin, et al. The cognitive neuroscience of the teacher–student interaction, *Mind, Brain, and Education*, 2013, 7 (3), 177–81, https://doi.org/10.1111/mbe.12025 (archived at https://perma.cc/KZR6-AU99)

20 N Yannier. Active learning: 'Hands-on' meets 'minds-on', *Science*, 2021, 374 (6563), 26–30, https://doi.org/10.1126/science.abj9957 (archived at https://perma.cc/MQ2E-WPDY)

21 J G M Kooloos, E M Bergman, M A G P Scheffers, et al. The effect of passive and active education methods applied in repetition activities on the retention of anatomical knowledge, *Anatomical Sciences Education*, 2019, 13 (4), 458–66, https://doi.org/10.1002/ase.1924 (archived at https://perma.cc/L3ZZ-ADUU)

22 K A Nguyen, M Borrego, C J Finelli, et al. Instructor strategies to aid implementation of active learning: A systematic literature review, *International Journal of STEM Education*, 2021, 8 (1), https://doi.org/10.1186/s40594-021-00270-7 (archived at https://perma.cc/VNP7-QAZY)

23 L Deslauriers, L S McCarty, K Miller and G Kestin. Measuring actual learning versus feeling of learning in response to being actively engaged in the classroom, *Proceedings of the National Academy of Sciences*, 2019, 116 (39), 19251–7, https://doi.org/10.1073/pnas.1821936116 (archived at https://perma.cc/YAF3-FNYR)

24 P Reuell. Study shows that students learn more when taking part in classrooms that employ active-learning strategies, *Harvard Gazette*, 5 September 2019, https://news.harvard.edu/gazette/story/2019/09/study-shows-that-students-learn-more-when-taking-part-in-classrooms-that-employ-active-learning-strategies/ (archived at https://perma.cc/QQ9Q-V2AW)

25 S Tharayil, M Borrego, M Prince, et al. Strategies to mitigate student resistance to active learning, *International Journal of STEM Education*, 2018, 5 (1), https://doi.org/10.1186/s40594-018-0102-y (archived at https://perma.cc/77H7-DN2R)

26 R Felder. How about a quick one? *Education for Chemical Engineers*, 1992, 26 (1, Winter), 18–19, www.engr.ncsu.edu/wp-content/uploads/drive/1ONUEg-44JZ_bQDKllhhDVFV02OEeK9KQ/1992-r_quickone.pdf (archived at https://perma.cc/7EDH-CBV7)

27 P Armbruster, M Patel, E Johnson and M Weiss. Active learning and student-centered pedagogy improve student attitudes and performance in introductory biology, *CBE – Life Sciences Education*, 2009, 8 (3), 203–13, https://doi.org/10.1187/cbe.09-03-0025 (archived at https://perma.cc/7U8F-2EZP)

28 R Felder and R Brent. Active learning: An introduction, *ASQ Higher Education Brief*, 2009, 2 (4, August), www.engr.ncsu.edu/wp-content/uploads/drive/1XaOo9WCKcMq6-fTcQGidOT2SDGqg70l5/2009-ALpaper(ASQ).pdf (archived at https://perma.cc/PB7P-35VT)

29 D A Lake. Student performance and perceptions of a lecture-based course compared with the same course utilizing group discussion, *Physical Therapy*, 2001, 81 (3), 896–902, https://doi.org/10.1093/ptj/81.3.896 (archived at https://perma.cc/4NXX-STCR)

30 L Deslauriers, L S McCarty, K Miller and G Kestin. Measuring actual learning versus feeling of learning in response to being actively engaged in the classroom, *Proceedings of the National Academy of Sciences*, 2019, 116 (39), 19251–7, https://doi.org/10.1073/pnas.1821936116 (archived at https://perma.cc/YAF3-FNYR)

31 D Leonard. Why organizations need to make learning hard, *Harvard Business Review*, 11 January 2016, https://hbr.org/2015/11/why-organizations-need-to-make-learning-hard (archived at https://perma.cc/CF6F-LUYS)

32 L Saunders and M A Wong (2020) *Instruction in Libraries and Information Centers*, Windsor & Downs Press, Urbana, https://doi.org/10.21900/wd.12 (archived at https://perma.cc/Y7YX-RT8B)

33 M Ng and T M Newpher. Comparing active learning to team-based learning in undergraduate neuroscience, *Journal of Undergraduate Neuroscience Education*, 28 June 2020, 18 (2), A102–A111, PMID: 32848518, PMCID: PMC7438168

34 M Ng and T M Newpher. Comparing active learning to team-based learning in undergraduate neuroscience, *Journal of Undergraduate Neuroscience Education*, 28 June 2020, 18 (2), A102–A111, PMID: 32848518, PMCID: PMC7438168

35 S Mitra. The Hole in the Wall project and the power of self-organised learning, Edutopia, 3 February 2012, www.edutopia.org/blog/self-organized-learning-sugata-mitra (archived at https://perma.cc/4YC7-XYYG)

36 C Cadwalladr. The 'granny cloud': The network of volunteers helping poorer children learn, *Guardian*, 2 August 2015, www.theguardian.com/education/2015/aug/02/sugata-mitra-school-in-the-cloud (archived at https://perma.cc/6K5C-TXRW)

5

Territorial, defensive, siloed

A story of everything wrong with prescriptive top-down learning as we know it

In previous chapters, we've charted the pivot in organizational learning away from content to people, offered a crash course in the childhood and rocky adolescence of e-learning, and outlined the science behind our blueprint for what learners really crave: stimulating social experiences driven by collaborative learning that help people upskill from within. All of that may be well and good, I hear you saying, but what does this really mean for individual learners?

Now let's break things down with a real story of why our old top-down learning culture simply can't give people the support they need to follow their curiosity, learn from others and contribute their own knowledge and expertise to benefit the collective.

Here's a cautionary tale of everything wrong with prescriptive learning as we know it. This is 'Dave's' story.

CASE STUDY
Let's call him Dave

We're about to dive into some unsavoury parts of traditional learning and development culture, not to mention a few examples of less-than-inspiring leadership, so we'll need a moniker for our protagonist. Let's call him Dave. Dave (not his real name) now works for 360Learning, where he's helping the team realize our vision for upskilling from within through collaborative learning. But this isn't about where Dave is now. It's about where he started.

In Dave's first job out of university, he found himself in a strange and unenviable position. He was working as a junior analyst for a government ministry in charge of developing and implementing social spending policy, and one of his early tasks was to contribute to the drafting of legislation setting out his country's annual expenditure on specific kinds of social support: tax credits for families with young children, accommodation stipends for low-income households, that sort of thing. At just a year or two out of university, Dave wasn't an expert in developing legislation by any means. But he was lucky enough to be paired with some experienced advisors, including some chief analysts who had written and promulgated thousands of pages of legislation between them.

These chief analysts showed Dave the basics: how to turn economic, legal and policy analysis into advice and recommendations for government ministers and committees; how to consult with key stakeholders in the social services sector; how to work with the legislative drafting office to make sure his draft bills had their intended effects and didn't cause any problems anywhere else in the complicated machinery of government; and how to shepherd these projects through a department replete with interpersonal tensions and administrative fiefdoms that would've made Kafka take a deep breath.

With his first few social policy spending bills drafted, debated and adopted, Dave became more and more comfortable with the legislative process. And as the chief advisors, who had been helping him, started to retire or move on to other ministries, more people started looking to Dave for help with their own legislative projects. Even though Dave had been in the job for only a handful of years, he'd developed the kind of first-hand experience that is hard to come by in government, and this made him a valuable source of advice and guidance.

This is where things got strange.

'If we start helping them, soon we'll be helping everybody'

It goes without saying that not every business, organization or government department has a positive, benevolent or enabling workplace culture. Whether it's a question of inadequate support for managers, insufficient resources to cover top operational priorities or simply a history of allowing dysfunctional or unproductive leadership to go unchecked, people can make some unfair and even baffling decisions at work. Or so Dave found, anyway.

At one of his weekly check-ins, Dave happened to mention to his manager the steady trickle of advisors from across the ministry coming to him for advice on all legislative questions big and small. What format did this submission document need to follow? How could someone expedite the timeframe for this bill or that bill? What do government ministers most want to see in a first reading speech? These were the kinds of niche questions that can be tough to find answers to, and Dave was only too happy to help out. He was still able to deliver on his other projects, and the questions were, for the most part, completely reasonable. It felt good, too – Dave was making a meaningful impact in the quality and consistency of the legislative projects his colleagues were advancing, and helping them to avoid the kinds of simple mistakes and omissions that can cause delays and confusion.

Dave's manager listened attentively before responding. It sounded like Dave was doing far too much for those other advisors, she said. His heart was in the right place, but it was time to get real about the situation. As reasonable as his colleagues' questions might be, it wasn't Dave's job to be the legislation guru for the whole ministry. After all, if Dave started helping them, soon he'd be helping everybody. And then where would he be?

As you might imagine, Dave didn't agree with his manager. But, being relatively new, he didn't want to rock the boat, either. So, he went along with her call. But still, the other advisors kept coming by to ask him questions about this bill or that bill. Wanting to help, and hating to shut the door in their faces, Dave suggested they email him instead. This way, rather than risking the ire of his manager, Dave could offer advice and suggestions without being too obvious about it. So, he kept on providing this clandestine support – strictly over email – for the next year or so, until he found an opportunity to shift into a different government ministry. All up, it never took more than a few hours of his time each week – hardly enough of a commitment to make a big difference to his output, but enough that he had to work a little harder to deliver against his wider projects.

It wasn't until he'd settled into his new job that Dave paused to ask himself whether this arrangement was normal. Was his manager right to put her team's core output first, at the expense of wider departmental learning? Surely it wasn't her responsibility to help a team member become the go-to source of information for the whole department, right? If she wasn't to blame for him having to help people in secret, then who was?

Who's really to blame – and how we can all do better

Unfortunately, stories like Dave's are more common than we'd like to admit. In pretty much every industry, sector and field, subject-matter experts are asked to share their knowledge and expertise to help projects succeed outside their own direct field of responsibility. The difference between Dave's situation and how the same circumstances would have been handled in a more benevolent and enabling work culture comes down to organization, resources and the right philosophy of learning. In other words, are the Daves of the world given the time, space and resources they need to share their know-how? Or are they encouraged to just eat what's on their plate and let the opportunity pass, with all that expertise staying locked up in their brains?

Besides the boilerplate managerial defensiveness and siloed approach to task allocation, there's a much bigger factor at play in Dave's story: time. If it takes every subject-matter expert like Dave hours out of his or her week to share knowledge and help others ramp up on specialist tasks like this, then why would anyone ever volunteer to help out? If you risk drawing the ire of a manager focused just on shipping core projects, then of course you'll stick to the basics, keep your know-how to yourself and let someone else worry about the learning opportunities. Forget upskilling from within – you're just in the job to do the basics and go home.

Let's think about the alternatives for a second. If you can give someone like Dave – and every other subject-matter expert out there – the tools they need to quickly build a course showcasing what they know, then iterate on this course with feedback and input from others, you can cut out all the repetition, ambiguity and secrecy Dave had to deal with. Instead of providing advice to people one at a time, Dave could have taken a day or two to create a foundational course on legislative drafting. It wouldn't have been perfect right away, because nothing ever is. But it would have captured a lot of the basic questions the other advisors kept coming to him to ask: speechwriting, document formatting, dos and don'ts for working with the drafting office, the fundamentals of statutory interpretation. Then, with the help of each of the other learners, Dave could have perfected it over time. Even better, he could have called everyone's attention to it, letting his colleagues know exactly where to go to find the answers they need, rather than having to hear about the legislation guru by word of mouth alone.

This might sound overly optimistic, but it doesn't have to be. All it takes is the right foundation of benevolent, peer-based learning, and a commitment to giving subject-matter experts the time and resources they need to solve common problems without having to put their own projects, mental health or prospects for promotion on the line.

Fortunately, Dave is now past these kinds of questions at 360Learning – or at least, I hope he is. We try to make it as easy and painless as possible for subject-matter experts to capture their expertise in response to shared problems, build courses their colleagues love, and iterate to make these courses even better over time. But creating this kind of culture isn't easy – it takes a daily commitment at every level to succeed. For now, let's leave Dave where he is, and take a look at how collaborative learning can enhance all the things that make your company culture great.

6

Collaborative learning as a culture enhancer

Innovation is the lifeblood of any successful organization. Show me a business leader who doesn't value and promote innovation, and I will show you a business that won't survive in the long run. But as with so many aspects of an organization that can't be captured on a balance sheet, identifying and cultivating the levers that drive innovation in an organization are easier said than done. While oceans of ink have been spilled in countless books and articles about the secrets of fostering innovation, their advice can all be condensed into a single word: talent.

The idea that skilled labour is the *sine qua non* of innovation may seem painfully obvious. No one would expect football hooligans to win the World Cup any more than they'd expect a group of car mechanics to build a rocket that could place someone on the moon. While the people in each of these groups undoubtedly have their own talents, they may not be particularly relevant to achieving goals that fall outside their domain of expertise. While hooligans and car mechanics might be extreme examples, they are meant to underscore the fact that the domain-relevant talent of an organization's employees is the single largest determining factor when it comes to achieving breakthroughs and driving innovation.

This is why all successful business leaders strive to build an organization that employs the best and the brightest in their field. They achieve this in two main ways: hiring talented employees from other organizations and developing the talents of their existing employees. The problem is that attracting and retaining talent has become more challenging than ever. As we've seen throughout this book, technological and socioeconomic trends have created severe headwinds for businesses when it comes to building a skilled workforce. Baby Boomers with decades of experience are retiring from the workforce at accelerating rates and taking vast amounts of hard-won knowledge with them on their way out.[1] Nearly one in five Millennials – who make up the next largest segment of the workforce after Boomers – switch jobs each year.[2] At the same time, the rise of remote work has opened up the limited pool of skilled labour to the global market, which means businesses have to fight harder than ever to hire and keep their best employees.

The combined force of these three factors – talent retirement, talent churn and talent globalization – has had a severe impact on organizational innovation. A recent survey found that more than half of companies globally are reporting talent shortages, which marks the highest level in more than a decade. The talent crisis is particularly acute in the United States, where talent shortages have tripled since 2010 and nearly two-thirds of businesses report that they are struggling to fill their positions.[3] For many organizations, this has converted talent acquisition from an item on their HR team's to-do list to a matter of existential importance for the business. Although the methods that are used to attract and retain talent will depend on the organization, a strong company culture usually turns out to be the best indicator of whether the company will be successful in its endeavour. In particular, organizations that build a culture around learning and leveraging internal expertise – in other words, upskilling from within – have proven that they are better able to retain talent and outperform their competitors.

What we talk about when we talk about culture

Before we dive into the mechanics of building a strong learning culture in an organization, it's worthwhile contemplating what we're actually talking about when we talk about an organization's culture. Although successful organizations have always touted their company culture as a selling point for employees, investors and customers, culture nevertheless remains a notoriously challenging concept to define in the abstract. The first person to make an attempt at formalizing the definition of a company's culture was a psychoanalyst-turned-management-consultant named Elliott Jaques in the early 1950s. In his pathfinding book, *The Changing Culture of a Factory*, Jaques defined a company's culture as 'its customary and traditional way of thinking and doing of things, which is shared to a greater or lesser degree by all its members, and which new members must learn, and at least partially accept, to be accepted into service in the firm'.[4]

It's not a bad start. At the most basic level, an organization's culture can be thought of as 'the way we do things'. But the simplicity of this definition is deceiving. Culture shapes and is shaped by every aspect of an organization, from the way that leaders communicate with their employees to the way that new employees are onboarded into the company. Culture sets employee expectations about their work and career prospects, it dictates the tone of customer interactions and shapes the values and behaviour of everyone in the organization. Culture is the skeleton that provides the scaffolding for all the other vital processes of a company, which is why it is so critically important for business leaders to get right.

This begs the question: what are the characteristics of a strong company culture? A recent article co-written by Boris Groysberg, a professor at Harvard Business School, outlined four crucial attributes of robust organization cultures based on an extensive overview of the research on the topic.[5] First and foremost, culture is shared. It is inherently a group phenomenon and cannot be driven by a CEO or any single person within an organization. Second, culture is pervasive. It is not siloed within any single department of an organization and should be understood by everyone from the mailroom to the C-suite. Third, culture is enduring. Culture is not created by hosting a company retreat once a year, but instead is something that emerges over time and can last for years, if not decades. Finally, culture is implicit. This doesn't mean that the tenets of a company's culture should be left unsaid, but that an organization's culture should be apparent to everyone even if it hasn't been explicitly stated. It shines through in the work they do, the way employees interact with each other, and so on.

There are many different pathways to building a company culture that has these attributes. Yet time and time again, management experts have found that fostering a *learning* culture is the most effective way for organizations to leverage culture to achieve their goals. As a report from Gallup put it, 'we have seen a clear trend toward prioritizing learning to promote innovation and agility as businesses respond to increasingly less predictable and more complex environments'.[6] The most successful businesses today and in the future will be those that fundamentally reorient their culture toward one that champions continuous learning at every level of the organization.

But what *is* a learning culture, anyway? Peter Senge, a senior lecturer at MIT Sloan who popularized the idea of learning cultures in his best-selling book on management, *The Fifth Discipline*, defined organizations that inherently embrace learning as places 'where people continually expand their capacity to create the results they truly desire, where new and expansive patterns of thinking are nurtured, where collective aspiration is set free, and where people are continually learning how to learn together'.[7]

Given this rather idealistic – although eminently practical, as we'll soon see – conception of a learning culture, it is perhaps unsurprising that companies that embrace this model are particularly effective at attracting and retaining talent. A recent survey found that the majority of Millennial job seekers report that the opportunity to learn and grow is 'extremely important' when applying for a job.[8] While learning and development opportunities are also important for Gen Xers and Baby Boomers, the data suggests they don't consider it to be as big of a determining factor of where they work as Millennials do. This makes sense given that Millennials are earlier in their career and are constantly on the look-out for opportunities to level up their skills to achieve success and stability in their professional lives.

The urgent question for business leaders and L&D professionals is how to establish a learning culture in their organization that is both impactful and enduring, and allows people to share their knowledge and help everyone upskill from within.

How collaborative learning enhances culture

As we've seen throughout this book, not all learning systems are created equal. The proliferation of tech-driven learning systems explored earlier in the book – LXPs, LMS, SCORM, and so on – clearly shows that organizations understand the value of a robust learning culture and are eager for tools to help them build it. But until the advent of systems built around collaborative learning, most of these corporate learning initiatives fell flat.

It's impossible to build a robust learning culture on the shaky foundations of past approaches to L&D. Collaborative learning tools and processes, however, have most of the attributes that a learning culture requires. In fact, you could go so far as to say that every effective learning culture is inherently collaborative. Furthermore, collaborative learning is more than an antidote to the challenges that organizations face when it comes to hiring and retaining talent. It fundamentally enhances a company's culture, often in ways that are surprising and difficult to predict at the outset. Culture is an organic phenomenon that always evolves in spontaneous directions, even within the relatively controlled environment of an organization. Collaborative learning enables this spontaneity and growth while ensuring that an organization's culture develops in a positive direction that furthers the goals of the organization and its members. This is a remarkable and unique feature of collaborative learning and it's worth unpacking how it's so effective as a culture enhancer.

Leveraging experts

One of the defining features of collaborative learning systems is their 'bottom-up' approach to knowledge creation that turns an organization's experts into educators and empowers people to upskill from within. This has several important implications when it comes to culture. Since employees have access to the brightest thinkers in their organization on any given subject, they will develop a deeper understanding of the importance of their work and pride in the calibre of talent in their organization – including their own. Furthermore, turning to internal experts to improve learning outcomes ensures that both the experts and the people who are learning from them feel valued by the organization. As a recent Gallup survey put it, workers increasingly 'expect their managers to do more than just manage; they expect them to coach'.[9] This is critical for retaining talented employees once they've been hired. Whereas centralized learning systems are focused on specific organizational outcomes like upskilling that can make employees feel like a number in the L&D machine, expert-driven collaborative learning focuses on improving outcomes for the individual. Experts derive value from helping their peers succeed and non-expert learners benefit from top-tier knowledge that is always relevant to their work, both of which enhance the organization's culture.

Peer interaction

Collaborative learning is fundamentally about peer interaction. While experts play a guiding role in collaborative learning environments, it is the exchange of questions and feedback among learners that ultimately determines successful outcomes. When collaborative learning systems foster interactions that transcend departmental silos or organizational hierarchies, they foster a deep bond between employees at all levels of the organization. This ensures directional alignment across an organization, which is one of the most important reasons to build a strong culture in the first place. And by fostering interactions that are respectful yet challenging – in the sense of encouraging learners to constantly strive for improvement – collaborative learning builds team cohesion by giving all learners the gratifying feeling of helping their colleagues. Collaborative learning acts as a rising tide that lifts all boats and helps them weather choppy waters whenever they're encountered. That's the power of upskilling from within.

Meeting employee needs

Collaborative learning depends on tight feedback loops between learners, experts and management. This ensures that learning material is always updated and relevant to learner needs, but it also contributes significantly to a strong organizational culture. The reason for this is because employee needs exist along a spectrum ranging from basic needs (e.g. having the right tools to do their job) to individual needs (e.g. adequate work–life balance) to team needs (e.g. sufficient operational independence). By creating a culture where open communication and feedback are used to improve and meet learning needs, collaborative learning systems also foster communication and feedback in other areas of the organization, which ensures that employee needs that aren't explicitly about learning are met as well. This is especially important when it comes to meeting higher-level needs like career growth and skill development, which is often a determining factor in whether an employee stays at an organization or looks for better opportunities elsewhere.

Supporting other culture enhancers

A beautiful feature of collaborative learning systems is how they imbue all areas of an organization with a learning mentality. Far from being limited to teaching an explicit new skill or simplifying onboarding or other training processes, collaborative learning can support other culture enhancement initiatives at the same time as it furthers an organization's learning goals. The benefits of collaborative learning are especially apparent in the context of diversity, equity and inclusion (DEI) initiatives. Consider the importance of allyship in building an inclusive culture. Collaborative learning tools give an organization's employees the ability to share information about how to be an effective ally through self-education, which reduces the already substantial burden that many people of colour experience from the feeling of constantly being asked to educate their peers on important DEI subjects. At the same time, collaborative learning tools create channels to encourage peers and recognize their achievement in ways that further the goals of the organization's DEI programmes.

Seven steps to build a collaborative learning culture

Now that we've established the ways that collaborative learning enhances an organization's culture, it's time to consider actionable methods for building that culture. It's important to acknowledge that a collaborative learning culture is not built overnight. It can take months or years of sustained commitment to overhaul a company's culture. But the fruits of this effort will become apparent very quickly and be compounded over time. If a company's learning culture were plotted on a graph, the line wouldn't be linear, but exponential. The progress may feel slow at first, but as time goes on the pace of progress will accelerate until it becomes an unstoppable force that feels entirely natural.

The key to successfully building a collaborative learning culture is consistency and clarity. What this looks like in practice will vary from organization to organization, but my experience of watching hundreds of companies take the plunge and embrace a learning culture revealed seven primary levers that increase the likelihood of a successful cultural transition (see Figure 6.1):

1 **Create a learning culture mission statement:** To build an effective collaborative learning culture, it is essential that organizations ensure that everyone is on the same page. This means that one of the first orders of business is to create and share a mission statement that establishes the company's learning goals and clearly articulates how employees' efforts contribute toward fulfilling this goal. A learning culture mission statement also helps an organization to understand whether it is making progress toward its goal. Without a clear understanding of what the organization aims to achieve and how it will achieve it, leaders and their employees risk running in circles. This will create the illusion of learning, but the results of learning initiatives will fall short of desired outcomes.

FIGURE 6.1   Building a collaborative learning culture

1   Create a learning culture mission statement

2   Reward experimentation and risk-taking

3   Set learning OKRs

4   Encourage outside learning

5   Foster open dialogue

6   Ensure executive support

7   Offload learning directives from HR

2 **Reward experimentation and risk-taking:** A key component of collaborative learning is ensuring that learners are engaged and contributing to the learning process. This means that learners must feel safe venturing beyond their comfort zone. Failure is an inevitable part of learning something new, and the more challenging the learning material, the more likely failure becomes. As such, organizations must clearly communicate to their employees that failure is acceptable and part of the learning process. They can achieve this by rewarding experimentation and risk-taking. The forms this can take will vary from organization to organization and may run the gamut from congratulatory shout-outs on community messaging systems to more substantial rewards like cash bonuses for successful experiments. Managers must devise systems that simultaneously ensure that learners are accountable for the outcomes of their experiments without penalizing them if those experiments fail. One way to accomplish this is to require employees to produce 'post-mortem' reports of their experiments, regardless of whether they are a success or a failure. This ensures that, even in the event of a failure, the employee still maintains accountability and is able to reflect and learn from the experience.

3 **Set learning OKRs:** Building a learning culture is an ongoing commitment and there is a natural tendency for learning objectives to fall to the wayside unless they are carefully tracked and managed. Setting objectives and key results (OKRs) will create urgency around learning objectives by setting deadlines and communicating to employees that they are ultimately responsible for their learning outcomes. It's also critical for helping employees overcome the sense that the time they spend learning at work will get them in trouble, which is a common experience for companies in the midst of a transition to a learning culture. OKRs establish learning as a fundamental priority for the company and help employees get comfortable with the idea that learning is now part of the job. OKRs have the added benefit of helping break down larger learning goals into smaller and more manageable tasks. For example, if a learning goal is to have employees teach themselves a new piece of software, the OKR wouldn't be expressed as 'Master this software'.

Instead, it would be broken down into modules where each objective might be mastering a particular feature of that software.

4 **Encourage outside learning:** As we saw earlier in the book, humans are naturally hardwired to learn. Our propensity to create and share knowledge doesn't stop when we log off for the day and the organizations with the most successful learning cultures lean into this reality by explicitly encouraging outside learning. Usually this means the organization needs to put its money where its mouth is, providing provided stipends to its employees for educational materials such as books and classes that are relevant to their jobs and actively promoting this benefit. The investment in a budget for outside learning will pay for itself many times over both directly and indirectly. By nurturing employees' education beyond the office, organizations will help meet their needs for personal and professional growth. At the same time, the new knowledge that employees gain outside formal L&D channels will flow back into the organization, leading to new insights that fuel innovation. Finally, the peer-to-peer nature of collaborative learning ensures that the outside knowledge that employees bring into the organization will flow to their peers and improve the learning experience for everyone in the company.

5 **Foster open dialogue:** Collaborative learning critically depends on the open exchange of ideas. Learners must be able to express their understanding of a new concept in a forum that promotes constructive feedback. In practice, this means that each employee should have the opportunity to offer their personal perspective on whatever challenge their team is trying to solve or their experience with a particular piece of educational material. This can be facilitated through formal assessments or feedback systems built into a collaborative learning tool or through more informal channels like group debriefs after a project. By allowing everyone to share their own thoughts, it enhances the learning culture by providing the entire group with a sense of how their peers think about a challenge, which can help identify blind spots or opportunities that may have been missed otherwise.

6 **Ensure executive support:** No one person in an organization can dictate its culture. At the same time, however, establishing a robust collaborative learning culture cannot be achieved without the full and unwavering support of executives and upper management. This goes beyond lip service to the ideals of collaborative learning. Instead, executives must lead by example. An organization's leaders should publicly announce their own learning goals to the organization and hold themselves accountable to their employees for meeting them. At the same time, they should demonstrate that the culture they're trying to build isn't about how much someone knows, it's about how willing they are to learn. This means a willingness to ask questions and to defer to experts within their organization whenever appropriate. In a strong collaborative learning culture, *everyone* is engaged in learning, regardless of whether it's the CEO or a summer intern.

7 **Offload learning directives from HR:** Collaborative learning is fundamentally a 'bottom-up' approach to knowledge creation. It stands in stark contrast to the top-down approaches of the past that were largely led by L&D teams and HR professionals. In the top-down arrangement, learning is perceived as a part of a company's business strategy rather than its culture. This often reduces it to a set of measurable outputs that may have little connection to the learning needs of employees. By taking learning directives out of the HR department and putting them into the hands of employees themselves, organizations ensure that learning is baked into the company's culture. It's something that everyone in the organization participates in and contributes to, rather than a directive given from the top. This also empowers HR and L&D professionals to transform their roles into coaches and mentors who facilitate the organic learning needs of the company's employees. For organizations that seek to build a robust collaborative learning culture, they must heed the immortal words of the management guru Peter Drucker: 'Culture eats strategy for breakfast.'

These seven techniques are a useful starting place for any organization setting off on the path toward an enduring culture of upskilling from within through collaborative learning. As organizations find their stride, they will adapt and add to these strategies to fit their own goals. It's important to remember that, while these strategies are necessary requirements for a collaborative learning culture, they are likely not sufficient. Building this culture is a lot like learning itself, insofar as it requires continual iteration based on critical appraisals of successes and setbacks faced along the way. It is also critically important for organizations to consider how these techniques will be experienced by individual employees during the learning process, which is where we'll turn our attention in the next chapter.

Notes

1 R Fry. The pace of boomer retirements has accelerated in the past year, Pew Research Center, 10 November 2020, www.pewresearch.org/fact-tank/2020/11/09/the-pace-of-boomer-retirements-has-accelerated-in-the-past-year (archived at https://perma.cc/3LXB-RQFC)

2 Gallup. How Millennials want to work and live, Gallup, 7 December 2021, www.gallup.com/workplace/238073/millennials-work-live.aspx (archived at https://perma.cc/R7W3-HV59)

3 C Castrillon. Why US talent shortages are at a 10-year high, Forbes, 28 September 2021, www.forbes.com/sites/carolinecastrillon/2021/09/22/why-us-talent-shortages-are-at-a-ten-year-high/?sh=46ed77df79c2 (archived at https://perma.cc/74CQ-3XWF)

4 E Jaques (1951) *The Changing Culture of a Factory*, Tavistock Press, London

5 B Groysberg, J Lee, J Price and J Y-J Cheng. The leader's guide to corporate culture, *Harvard Business Review*, 2018, https://hbr.org/2018/01/the-leaders-guide-to-corporate-culture (archived at https://perma.cc/F6ZG-TNJX)

6 Gallup. Culture transformation, Gallup, nd, www.gallup.com/workplace/229832/culture.aspx (archived at https://perma.cc/4J65-CQFN)

7 P Senge (1990) *The Fifth Discipline*, Random House, London

8 Gallup. How Millennials want to work and live, Gallup, 7 December 2021, www.gallup.com/workplace/238073/millennials-work-live.aspx (archived at https://perma.cc/R7W3-HV59)

9 B Rigoni and J Asplund. Strengths-based development: The manager's role, Gallup, 6 October 2016, www.gallup.com/workplace/236369/strengths-based-development-manager-role.aspx (archived at https://perma.cc/FHX5-JVPR)

7

How upskilling from within through collaborative learning can guide the employee journey

Collaborative learning is at its core a human-driven knowledge production system. It is implemented in the context of organizations and leverages digital technologies, but without the support and engagement of learners it doesn't matter how good the content is or how often an executive reminds their employees of the importance of learning; it will fail to deliver results. As we saw in the previous chapter, making collaborative learning the foundation of an organization's culture is an important step toward achieving employee buy-in of this approach to people development. Still, it is important to remember that a company's culture is like the air we breathe. It is always all around us, but its ubiquity also means it has a tendency to fade into the background for employees. Just like we don't have to think about every breath we take, once an employee has accustomed themselves to an organization's culture they tend to stop thinking about it explicitly. They just go with the flow.

For organizations that have already established a robust collaborative culture, this is a fine result. The question is how to get there. The key is for L&D professionals to stop thinking about collaborative learning in the abstract and for executives to stop focusing only on the business outcomes of their collaborative learning system. Instead, they must examine the ways that collaborative learning affects their employees at each stage in their journey with the company. L&D teams should demonstrate the benefits of collaborative learning starting with their offer letter to a new employee and continue throughout their employment. This will ensure that collaborative learning continues to deliver results for both the organization and its employees. In this chapter we'll examine how upskilling from within through collaborative learning intersects with each stage of a typical employee journey.

Preboarding

Preboarding is the phase between when a new employee signs an offer letter and their first day on the job. It can range from a few days to a few months, but regardless of how long preboarding lasts, organizations shouldn't wait to start introducing their newest employees to the benefits of collaborative learning.

The first day at a new job is often both an exciting and a stressful time for employees. They're meeting new people, adjusting to an unfamiliar work setting, getting to know how the company operates and dealing with more prosaic matters like setting up their company laptop. Organizations can substantially reduce their employees' day one jitters by deploying collaborative learning tools to help get new hires up to speed before they've even started.

For example, access to all the relevant tools for their job is one of the most common challenges faced by new employees. Sometimes, simply finding out which tools are available can be a major struggle. These challenges are compounded if the tools are unfamiliar to the new employee, who must first find quality educational resources and then teach themselves how to use the tool. Resources created through the company's collaborative learning culture have a lot to offer this employee. Video tutorials explaining key company workflows or instructions on how to use a particular tool can be created by other employees and shared with the new hire before they even start.

While most organizations have some form of onboarding instructional material, the resources created by the employee's new peers are superior in a few ways to materials created by an HR team. First, they are created by people who have been in the new employee's shoes and understand what it's like to try to orient yourself at the company. They will have insights into particular pain points or unexpected challenges for new employees that HR may not be aware of. Furthermore, preboarding content created by the new employee's peers has a secondary function of helping them get to know their team. By the time they start, they will already have a sense of who their colleagues are and who is considered an expert in a given area, which will make it easier for the employee to get the help they need as they begin the onboarding process.

Onboarding

The onboarding process is one of the most crucial steps in integrating an employee into an organization's collaborative learning culture. This is because the experience an employee has during their first days and weeks at a new company can have a significant impact on their long-term success. Studies have shown that 20 per cent of employee turnover happens during their first 45 days on a job, and around 4 per cent of new hires leave their job following a disastrous first day. This can have a deep impact on an organization's bottom line, considering that an employee who leaves during their first year can cost a company more than three times that employee's salary in sunk training costs and lost productivity. As such, it's hardly a surprise that a recent survey from Deloitte found that 79 per cent of business leaders consider reforming their onboarding process to be an urgent priority.[1]

Collaborative learning can significantly improve onboarding outcomes by forcing executives and HR professionals to establish a structured process that goes beyond a simple checklist or instruction manual for new hires. They must consider all the points of ambiguity or confusion that can limit the effectiveness of existing onboarding processes and implement specific solutions for each potential roadblock. New hires are usually given an overwhelming amount of information during their first days on a job. They're effectively thrown in at the deep end and told to swim, but by intentionally crafting educational materials that are designed to address common challenges in a structured manner, organizations can throw their new hires a life jacket.

Importantly, using collaborative learning methods to structure the onboarding process is about more than removing barriers to employee success. It's also a great opportunity to show new hires the company's collaborative learning culture in action. This is the time for an organization's leadership to drop the sales pitch and prove that peer-driven education actually does drive employee success and increase job satisfaction. This can be a scary idea for leaders who are new to collaborative learning because there's nowhere to hide. The numbers on employee engagement, productivity and happiness won't lie. Fortunately, collaborative learning has a proven track record of improving all of these metrics for organizations that embrace it.

The form collaborative learning takes during onboarding should be tailored to the stage of the process. Generally speaking, onboarding can be divided into two distinct phases: induction and role-specific onboarding. Upskilling from within plays a key role in both phases.

Induction is a time for organizations to show their new hires the fundamentals of the business. They will learn about its products or services, how the organization creates value for clients, what the company culture is like, and who's who in the organization. Understanding the foundation of the business is key to a new hire's success, but it can also be hard for them to orient themselves in a strange new environment. This is where the collective expertise that is fundamental to collaborative learning comes into play. When organizations embrace collaborative learning, they rely on experts in each department to create educational content that will empower colleagues on their own team, in addition to educating employees in other parts of the company about the work they do. This is the power of upskilling from within through collaborative learning: it's intrinsically a cross-team exercise in knowledge creation, which proves especially useful when a new employee needs to get up to speed on the internal mechanics of an organization. They'll be able to draw upon a wealth of learning material – most of which is not created specifically for onboarding – to orient themselves and attain a deep understanding of the roles that different departments play within the organization.

Once an employee has the general lie of the land at their new company, they typically move into role-specific onboarding. During this phase, employees move beyond the basics of the company and begin to learn about the specific activities they'll engage in, how their performance will be evaluated, and how they will interact with their teammates to get the job done. This is the phase where the mentorship model at the core of collaborative learning really shines. While collaborative learning places L&D leaders into a coach or mentor role, they tend to operate on a company-wide basis to help teams achieve their learning goals. Yet this same model can also be adopted within each individual team or department to establish mentors for both new and existing employees. A study by the Human Capital Institute, a consultancy for HR professionals, found that 87 per cent of organizations that incorporated a mentor or buddy system into their onboarding process saw improvements in the proficiency of their new employees.[2] When organizations fully embrace a collaborative learning culture, mentorship is built into the learning system itself. That means there is no need for HR to stand up an entirely new buddy system – this is how the organization teaches and learns by default.

Ramp up

After an employee has learned the fundamentals of the company and their role, they typically enter a ramp-up period. During this time, the new employee is expected to show increasing proficiency in their role and eventually hit full productivity. The ramp-up period can vary from a few weeks to several months, depending on the demands of the employee's position. With collaborative learning systems in place, executives and L&D pros can be sure that the employee is learning their job as thoroughly and efficiently as possible during this crucial time.

One of the most important features of collaborative learning systems during the ramp-up period is the emphasis on daily learning practices. Unlike top-down learning systems that typically are built around scheduled one-off training, collaborative systems emphasize continuous learning. Collaborative learning platforms accomplish this by giving new employees daily learning tasks that are designed to improve their core competencies. This makes learning complex work-flow processes simple by breaking down a large topic into digestible chunks, while simultaneously giving them a straightforward metric for evaluating their progress. No one becomes an expert in a new area overnight, but collaborative learning systems allow new hires to learn at their own pace while providing a roadmap of what they need to learn to go from being a novice to being an expert.

Promotion

For many employees, the process of internal promotion in their company can feel opaque and arbitrary. This can lead to decreased employee satisfaction and greater employee turnover. This makes establishing a clear pathway for promotion one of the most impor-tant levers a company has for retaining talent and fostering employee growth. But without a collaborative learning system in place, HR professionals still struggle to find adequate objective metrics to serve as a foundation for internal promotion. This is especially true in knowledge industries, where evaluating an individual employee's contribution to a team project can be a difficult task given the intan-gible nature of many inputs to an endeavour. They are ultimately beholden to the judgements of an employee's direct manager, which is an imperfect system that invites all kinds of (un)intentional distortions.

While collaborative learning can't completely eliminate the chal-lenges with creating an objective method for promoting employees within an organization, it can offer a second set of highly reliable criteria for judging an employee's performance. These criteria are based on the employee's contributions to the company's learning culture. If the employee is creating educational materials that are well received by their peers, asking the organization's experts insightful questions, and answering other questions for their peers, this is a strong indicator that they have mastered their role and are a great candidate for promotion. At the same time, collaborative learning actively helps employees advance their career by cultivating leadership skills – teaching, listening, providing constructive feedback – that are necessary to thrive at higher levels in the organization.

Lateral progression

Of course, vertical progression up the company ladder is not the only move an employee might make on their journey in a company. Many employees also experience lateral career moves either by choice or by circumstance. A striking example of this in practice was all the firms that had to quickly reskill large pools of their workforce in response to the Covid-19 pandemic. Consider the case of Malaysia Airlines, which offered thousands of flight attendants and pilots the opportunity to develop skills in other areas like facilities management when the foundation of their business crumbled after people stopped travelling.[3] In other cases, organizations – especially technology companies – embrace lateral movement as part of their internal culture. For example, lateral career moves are so common at Google that the company set up an internal job board and formal process to help employees find new opportunities within the company.[4] And finally, employees themselves often request a lateral move within an organization to seek out new challenges and develop new skills.

Collaborative learning is incredibly helpful to facilitating lateral movements within a company without causing major disruptions. This is largely the result of its emphasis on cross-departmental education and its reliance on internal experts to craft learning materials that are relevant to employees. If an employee is toying with the idea of transferring to a new department, they can prepare themselves for this change by immersing themselves in the educational material produced by that department. They can engage with subject-matter experts to test their understanding of what that new role will require while simultaneously getting to know the team and building a basic level of proficiency that will ease the transition. A crucial aspect of collaborative learning in this respect is that it is perfectly scalable. So whether it's one employee looking to shake up their career or a company that needs to reskill hundreds of employees basically overnight, collaborative learning platforms are up to the task.

Expanding expertise

Research shows that employee engagement at a firm follows a predictable path based on the length of time that an employee spends at a company. On average, an employee's engagement is highest during their first year and gradually fades over the next few years before bottoming out around an employee's fifth anniversary with the company. But if the employee continues on with the company, something remarkable happens: their engagement levels start to rise again. This phenomenon, which some commentators have called the 'tenure curve', reveals a critically important fact about the role of expertise in shaping employee outcomes.[5] In particular, it shows that increasing expertise and employee engagement are highly correlated. This assumes that the length of time an employee spends in an organization corresponds to greater domain expertise, but I don't think this assumption is too much of a stretch. After all, if an employee doesn't become significantly more knowledgeable about their work after a decade on the job, odds are they aren't going to make it to their 10-year anniversary anyway.

It's hardly surprising that employees become more engaged as they gain expertise. It is often more satisfying to work in an area where you have a deep knowledge base compared to an area where you know little to nothing. As the tenure curve demonstrates, the novelty of a new subject to master fades fast. Experience gives experts the ability to identify new challenges or opportunities that would go undetected by a dilettante and find delight in the all-too-familiar. But what can executives and L&D professionals *do* with this information? My takeaway is that organizations need to cultivate expertise in their employees as rapidly as possible. This will ensure they quickly pass through the trough of low engagement experienced by employees who are competent at what they do, but not yet experts.

In terms of turning employees into experts, collaborative learning systems are unparalleled. The reason for this is because collaborative learning systems are inherently expert-driven. They connect learners with the best and the brightest minds within their organization, and these experts help teach them the skills they need to advance their careers and find solutions to the challenges they face daily in their job. Leveraging internal experts with collaborative learning systems is like giving your employees the opportunity to have Lionel Messi teach you football or Shakespeare teach you poetry. They're always learning from the best. Moreover, collaborative learning systems emphasize tight feedback loops that ensure that learners are able to constantly test their understanding of a subject and build proficiency faster. Finally, collaborative learning systems also give employees the opportunity to teach their peers, and countless studies have shown the incredible learning benefits that come when people teach others a subject they are trying to master themselves.[6]

By leveraging the power of upskilling from within through collaborative learning during every stage of an employee's journey in an organization, executives and L&D leaders can promote employee satisfaction and improve engagement, all while boosting the organization's productivity and enhancing its culture. It's a sweet deal, but not without its challenges. In the next chapter we'll identify some common roadblocks that reduce the effectiveness of collaborative learning, and show you how to overcome them.

Notes

1   Bersin by Deloitte. Bersin by Deloitte research: Strategic onboarding can help new hires 'get off on the right foot' and provide an on-ramp to long-term employee success, Cision PR Newswire, 23 October 2014, www.prnewswire. com/news-releases/bersin-by-deloitte-research-strategic-onboarding-can-help-

new-hires-get-off-on-the-right-foot-and-provide-an-on-ramp-to-long-term-
employee-success-746324006.html (archived at https://perma.cc/48TW-FXGW)

2 Zavvy. How and why to create an onboarding buddy program, Zavvy, 2022,
www.zavvy.io/blog/onboarding-buddy-program (archived at https://perma.cc/
D8VV-Y8NP)

3 Malaysia Airlines. Malaysia Aviation Group offers employees the opportunity to
reskill for a better future, Malaysia Airlines, 2020, www.malaysiaairlines.com/
id/id/news-article/2020/malaysia-aviation-group-offers-reskill-better-future.html
(archived at https://perma.cc/A9M8-2QPM)

4 C Clee. Internal mobility: Switching roles at Google, Google, 21 June 2019,
https://blog.google/inside-google/life-at-google/internal-mobility-switching-
roles-a (archived at https://perma.cc/LA5K-QY5H)

5 K Ryba. Keeping tenured employees engaged: How tenure impacts engagement,
Quantum Workplace, 2020, www.quantumworkplace.com/future-of-work/
keeping-tenured-employees-engaged (archived at https://perma.cc/B5A8-8TR8)

6 I Gersch. It's not what you learn – it's how you learn! BPS, 12 June 2018,
www.bps.org.uk/psychologist/its-not-what-you-learn-its-how-you-learn
(archived at https://perma.cc/36XL-VVAA)

8

Common obstacles to realizing the value of collaborative learning – and how to overcome them

Throughout this book we've explored the many ways organizations can create value through upskilling from within through collaborative learning. Still, it's natural for leaders to feel some trepidation at the thought of transitioning to a new learning culture – even when they recognize the immense rewards of overhauling their approach to knowledge creation. In my experience working with organizations ranging from fledgling startups to titans of industry, I've found that there are several key concerns that are shared by leaders and L&D professionals regardless of the size of their organization, its industry or its existing approach to people development. While their concerns are valid and can certainly block the successful implementation of collaborative learning if they are not addressed, they are all totally manageable provided there is the right level of support, dedication and patience within the organization.

In this chapter we'll explore six common roadblocks that organizations face when upskilling from within through collaborative learning – and how to address them. Before we dive in, however, there is a general observation that is worth keeping in mind as an organization prepares to shift from top-down learning to a collaborative learning system.

The first is that creating a culture of collaborative learning is a gradual process. Leaders cannot and should not attempt to make the entire pivot overnight. The important thing to remember as the transition occurs is that collaborative learning is an ongoing commitment; it will not deliver results if it is implemented with a 'set and forget' mindset. In many ways, organizations never truly finish their transition to a collaborative learning system. Once the relevant tools and processes are set up, organizations constantly improve their mastery of collaborative learning techniques. While the adjustment to the new system may feel slow in the beginning, if it is implemented with a long-term outlook, the organization's leadership and L&D professionals will see the benefits of collaborative learning compound over time.

The second observation is that transitioning to collaborative learning doesn't require dismantling all existing people management processes and systems. Leaders often reject collaborative learning because they are in the grip of the sunk cost fallacy. After spending so much time, energy and capital establishing a top-down learning process, they are understandably reluctant to waste all that hard work – *even if it's not delivering the results they expected*. While collaborative learning is a fundamentally different approach to conventional learning systems in the sense that learning occurs bottom-up instead of top-down, it can still leverage existing resources and processes from pre-existing learning systems. For example, third-party learning content can still live alongside materials created by employees to create a robust educational ecosystem. It is critical that leaders at organizations considering a transition to collaborative learning understand that this new approach to L&D is meant to adapt existing learning structures rather than destroy them.

With these two general observations in mind, let's turn to six common obstacles that organizations may face as they build a culture of upskilling from within through collaborative learning.

Obstacle #1: Building stakeholders

A failure to build stakeholders is the most common reason why organizations fail to successfully integrate collaborative learning.

This is fundamentally a communication problem and is solved by early disclosure of an organization's intentions and transparency during the transition to the new learning system.

It is critical to build a broad base of stakeholders in any collaborative learning system because the success of the system ultimately depends on participation from an organization's employees. But L&D leaders should not attempt to get everyone on board all at once. The best pathway to success is to implement the new techniques one initiative or project at a time. The success with these projects will then make it easier to convince leaders in other departments to follow suit. Over time, L&D leaders will find that they have amassed broad support for this new approach to learning. The key is convincing those first few stakeholders to trust the L&D team in its efforts to provide meaningful support for their activities, rather than merely delivering content.

The needs of stakeholders will vary from organization to organization and it can be difficult for L&D teams to verify whether they are engaging stakeholders enough to ensure a successful transition to a collaborative learning culture. This is why it is critical to solicit feedback from throughout the organization during the transition. At a basic level, this allows L&D teams to answer questions from employees to help them become comfortable with the new system. It will also help identify gaps where employee needs are not being met so they can fix this and create engaged stakeholders.

Obstacle #2: Trusting learning priorities

The main reason that L&D teams and executives fear collaborative learning is because they perceive it as a total loss of control over an organization's learning process. They imagine their carefully crafted training processes devolving into anarchy and an overall destruction of knowledge within the organization. This common misperception is the result of unfamiliarity with the mechanics of collaborative learning, but even more fundamentally it stems from a lack of trust in an organization's employees to determine their own learning needs.

This often causes L&D teams and executives to cling to their old systems of control, which means that they're only able to partially implement a true collaborative learning system. This not only prevents them from experiencing the fruits of collaborative learning, it also makes their organizational learning system less effective as a whole. By failing to fully commit to collaborative learning, leaders become the main obstacle to their organization's success.

The best thing for leaders to do when it comes to establishing learning priorities under a collaborative learning system is to get out of the way and let the learners run the show. This is a radical departure from the top-down learning styles common to most organizations and as such it is critical that executives are allowed to ease into this new learning modality rather than being thrown in at the deep end. The first step is for L&D leaders to use data to identify points of failure within the learning culture and how these are affecting the organization. This is critically important because learners often don't know what their own learning needs are and need data themselves to understand their true development needs. Once L&D leaders have accomplished this, they must track metrics around employee engagement and the results of their learning. This will give executives a data-driven look at collaborative learning in action and reveal how allowing employees to take their education into their own hands dramatically boosts engagement and knowledge creation in the organization.

The transition to collaborative learning won't happen overnight, and it won't happen at all if an organization's leaders aren't allowed to slowly acclimatize themselves to the idea. One way to overcome this obstacle during the earliest phase of the transition is to begin with a single team within the organization. This team will essentially be a collaborative learning 'guinea pig' that will allow executives to see the new learning processes in action without having to worry about disrupting the entire organization. In this case, it's critical that L&D professionals engage the relevant team early in the process so they know what is expected of them and why their participation in the collaborative learning pilot programme is critical to the organization's L&D needs.

Obstacle #3: Embracing the new L&D team roles

It's not just executives who are wary of transitioning to upskilling from within through collaborative learning. L&D professionals have a lot at stake, too. The important thing for L&D teams to understand is that collaborative learning won't make them irrelevant, but it will dramatically change the nature of their jobs. Under the prescriptive learning paradigm that dominates organizational people development today, L&D teams are responsible for identifying the learning needs of employees, furnishing content that meets these needs and managing the distribution of learning materials throughout an organization. This requires soliciting educational materials from third-party platforms, scheduling courses, following up with learners on course completions, requesting feedback from learners and triaging training priorities based on the L&D team's beliefs about the organization's learning needs.

Under a collaborative learning system, the role of L&D teams dramatically changes. In addition to their role as strategic partners and product managers who are seeking out performance and capacity challenges, L&D leaders also become coaches and mentors who are primarily responsible for creating an environment where learning happens seamlessly between peers. They work to establish a collaborative learning environment that is designed to scale learning outcomes. As learners within the organization create more courses, the L&D team guides them through their learning experiences to ensure they're taking the right course and using the new system effectively. The ultimate goal of the L&D team in a collaborative learning environment is to create an agile learning system that can quickly respond to changing educational needs while still hitting the organization's learning goals, whether that's higher employee engagement or a large-scale reskilling programme.

In some instances, members of the L&D team may not act as coaches themselves. Instead, they will work with senior members of other teams to establish them as coaches. This approach tends to make sense in large organizations with thousands of employees, which would make it prohibitively difficult for an L&D team to play the role of coach and mentor for every other team in the organization. By delegating the coaching responsibility to project or team leads, L&D professionals can scale collaborative learning and focus on the role of being 'meta-coaches' who help team leaders excel in their new role as mentors for their peers.

Obstacle #4: Identifying learning needs

A frequent objection to collaborative learning is that it will make it difficult or impossible for L&D teams and executive leadership to identify the learning needs for their organization. Under conventional learning systems, L&D teams start with the objectives of the organization, identify areas where the organization is falling short of these goals, and then design training materials to enhance performance to achieve key objectives. The problem with this approach is that by the time the L&D team has gone through this process, the learning materials it produces may no longer match the learning needs of employees due to changing external circumstances, or the learning needs identified by the L&D team may never have aligned with the actual learning needs in the first place.

Collaborative learning overcomes this challenge by allowing employees to express their own learning needs while allowing their peers to create content that directly addresses those needs. This guarantees that learning content *always* corresponds to actual learner needs and is never out of date, because the learning cycle occurs in real time. Where organizations run into trouble is when L&D teams continue to dictate the needs of learners. In many cases, the way this happens is that an organization embraces bottom-up content creation and top-down content roadmaps simultaneously. For example, the L&D team might tell the sales department that it needs to create learning material on a new product. While this allows the sales team to create its own learning material, it may be the case that this content is not actually relevant to the team or is not the primary learning need of its members. This wastes time and resources without helping the organization advance toward its learning goals. Failure to identify learning needs is closely linked with the failure to trust employees to identify learning priorities. The remedy is simple. L&D leaders need to defer to the wisdom of the people who understand their learning needs best – the learners themselves – and empower them to articulate those needs based on data that links individual learning gaps with real challenges within the organization. Neither the L&D team nor the learners can achieve a collaborative learning culture on their own. They must help each other to identify skills gaps and implement learning solutions.

Obstacle #5: Maintaining the quality of learning resources

A common misconception about collaborative learning is that it inevitably leads to a deterioration in the quality of educational materials because there is 'no one in charge' to ensure that the content is kept to a minimum standard. In reality, the content created on peer-to-peer collaborative learning platforms maintains a high level of quality because it adheres to guidelines created by L&D teams. Part of the new role of L&D professionals in a collaborative learning environment is to establish a templated approach to content creation. This has two primary purposes. First, it ensures that the content on the platform is consistent and high quality. Second, it simplifies the process of creating the content, which encourages more employees to contribute to the collaborative learning system. Still, even with these guardrails in place, it will likely be necessary for L&D teams to periodically audit the content on their platform to verify that it is adhering to the established guidelines.

In order to maintain the quality of educational resources during the transition to a collaborative learning environment, it's critical that L&D leaders establish what constitutes high-quality content in the first place. In the past, the quality of content was easy to control through the selection of the third-party vendors that were responsible for producing it. They were professionals whose job was exclusively focused on creating educational content. In collaborative learning systems, however, learning materials are produced by employees whose primary job typically doesn't involve content creation. So while they may be knowledgeable in a particular area, that doesn't necessarily mean they will be competent at creating content that effectively conveys this knowledge to others. This is where L&D leaders can come in and guide the employee on methods for improving the effectiveness of their learning content. But first they need to be able to consistently identify sub-par content.

One of the most important ways for L&D teams to appraise the quality of a piece of content is to monitor feedback from other employees. Feedback loops are central to any effective collaborative learning ecosystem because they rapidly identify content that is out of date, inaccurate, or otherwise not up to an organization's standards. By allowing learners to comment on and react to learning materials, L&D professionals can easily identify pain points within their content ecosystem and help their colleagues implement fixes. Another core metric for L&D teams to keep an eye on is course completion rates. By assessing how many learners fail to finish a course once they've started it, L&D coaches can quickly find learning material that likely does not clear their quality threshold. Another great indicator of quality content is how often it is recommended to other learners. If no one is sharing a piece of content with their peers, it probably isn't that useful and needs to be improved or removed from the learning platform. Finally, L&D professionals can leverage self-assessments from learners who have completed a course to understand whether they think they will be able to apply the learning from the course to their job. This is the gold standard of high-quality collaborative learning content, and if learners consistently report that they don't think a course will be useful to them in their role it's unlikely that the course will pass a quality review check.

Obstacle #6: Engaging busy experts

When it comes to collaborative learning – indeed, to business in general – an organization's internal experts are the key to success. Much like the L&D team members, an organization's experts are expected to play the role of an educational mentor to their peers. But this can create challenges if the experts feel that creating learning content will create an undue burden that will distract them from working on whatever it is they happen to be an expert in. This is similar to a complaint often voiced by top professors in universities, who bemoan the fact that they must take time away from their research to give lectures to college freshmen on the basics of their field. In many universities, the solution to this conundrum was to foist teaching responsibilities onto adjunct professors and let the established professors focus on their research. While this may appease the professors, it also means the quality of the students' education declines because they are now learning from a relative novice in their field rather than a seasoned expert.

Organizations that are introducing collaborative learning should strive to avoid this outcome at all costs, which means finding ways to get experts to contribute learning content. A common failure mode for collaborative learning is when experts disengage and only relatively inexperienced employees contribute learning materials. While this is better than nothing at all, it is only marginally so because employees are not learning from the best in their area of work and thus are not reaching their full potential or growing in their career as fast as they would be if they were learning from the best of the best.

A key element of engaging busy experts in collaborative learning systems is to relentlessly reduce the friction involved with creating course material. While the speed of content creation is a feature of collaborative learning systems rather than an end in itself, it is critically important to the wider collaborative learning environment. The reason for this is because it will make it less likely that experts will see contributing to the collaborative learning system as a burden that distracts them from their 'real' work. In fact, a rather counterintuitive facet of collaborative learning systems is that the more successful they are, the *less* time employees will spend learning to achieve the same results. This is a result of the fact that employees tend to engage only with courses that are actually relevant to their needs (as opposed to whatever is prescribed by management) combined with courses created by experts who only provide information that their peers will find useful. Everyone involved with the system is highly incentivized to create and consume only relevant content; this 'trims the fat' in learning systems, and employees are able to achieve better learning outcomes in less time compared with conventional learning systems.

From learning challenges to opportunities

Collaborative learning presents a remarkable opportunity for organizations to improve their culture and business outcomes while simultaneously boosting employee engagement and advancing their careers. But establishing a robust collaborative learning culture is rarely easy.

Every organization is bound to encounter unexpected challenges as it works to establish a collaborative learning environment. The good news is that the feedback loops that are central to collaborative learning systems means these challenges will become smaller and more manageable over time as the organization learns to flex its collaborative muscles. In this respect, collaborative learning functions as a sort of meta-learning system that not only helps employees with first-order learning tasks that are directly relevant to their jobs, but also helps them become better learners and teachers. In this way, collaborative learning systems are constantly improving as a natural feature of the system, and the more that an organization embraces the collaborative learning model the more robust this organizational learning machine becomes. In the next chapter we'll look at how a few companies are upskilling from within through collaborative learning in their organizations today and what this can tell us about the future of this learning system.

9

How the world's leading experts are leveraging collective knowledge to solve impossible problems

The collaborative learning movement has reached an inflection point. Organizations around the world are embracing this new method of knowledge creation to overcome emerging challenges, seize opportunities resulting from unprecedented social, economic and technological disruptions and upskill from within. We've seen why collaborative learning is uniquely suited to helping organizations to stay nimble in the face of rapid change while improving their internal culture. But even if collaborative learning makes sense in the abstract, it's natural to wonder what this kind of learning system looks like in practice.

The forms that collaborative learning takes in the real world are as diverse as the organizations that implement it. While some features are found in every organization with a collaborative learning culture – engaged internal experts, self-directed learning, peer interactions – each organization will put its own spin on the system by emphasizing some features more than others. This is a reflection of the fact that every business has idiosyncratic needs and challenges. The beautiful thing about collaborative learning is that it functions like an educational Swiss army knife that can be adapted to any situation.

Earlier in this book, we saw how companies like AlphaSights transitioned to a culture of upskilling from within through collaborative learning to meet their organizational goals, whether that was improving the customer onboarding process or boosting employee satisfaction. In this chapter we'll take a look at how three established companies in very different industries – auto manufacturing, fast food and online search – have implemented a collaborative learning blueprint to overcome 'impossible' problems in their domain. These companies have been developing their collaborative learning culture for years and it has been a key input to their success. By examining what collaborative learning looks like in practice at some of the largest and most successful companies in the world, you'll gain a better understanding of how you can use collaborative learning in your own organization to deliver better L&D outcomes.

Tesla

Tesla is a company that hardly needs an introduction. The auto-maker's name has become synonymous with innovation due to its constant stream of breakthroughs in areas like electric vehicle manu-facturing, artificial intelligence and battery chemistry. In little over a decade, Tesla has grown from a scrappy startup selling luxury electric vehicles (EVs) to the most valuable car company in the world, a truly astonishing feat given the hyper-competitive and capital-intensive nature of the auto-manufacturing industry. The rise of Tesla is a David-versus-Goliath story if ever there was one, but it would never have been possible without a deep commitment to radically rethink-ing the way that knowledge flows throughout an organization.

Tesla's willingness to challenge the status quo is a core feature of the company's identity. As the company writes in its 'Anti-handbook handbook' for new employees, 'we're different and we like it that way'.[1] A hallmark of Tesla's unconventional culture is the extreme trust and responsibility it puts in its employees. Everyone at Tesla is expected not only to be a self-directed learner, but also to make suggestions about ways to improve the company whenever they see an opportunity. As new employees are told in the anti-handbook, 'your good ideas mean nothing if you keep them to yourself'.

The open exchange of knowledge is a critical feature of any strong collaborative learning programme. It also reflects Tesla's emphasis on leveraging internal experts. Tesla CEO Elon Musk is well known for his insistence on hiring the best and the brightest regardless of their academic pedigree. He cares less about whether a job candidate has the right degree than if they are intelligent and capable of putting their ideas into action. In this sense, Tesla considers all its employees to be experts regardless of whether they are a line worker or an executive. And, like experts in any collaborative learning environment, they are expected to share their ideas and knowledge with their peers.

Yet Musk also understands that *how* employee expertise is shared matters just as much as the information they are sharing. The rapid pace of innovation at Tesla requires knowledge to flow throughout the organization with minimal friction. This necessarily requires the type of peer-to-peer exchange that is central to upskilling from within, as opposed to the more conventional flow of information up and down a corporate hierarchy. In an all-staff email Musk sent in 2017, the 'Technoking' of Tesla made this mandate explicit. The flow of information through a rigid hierarchy, he wrote, is 'incredibly dumb'. Instead, 'anyone at Tesla can and should talk to anyone else... without anyone else's permission'.[2] The point of breaking down barriers between managers, employees and departments is to accelerate the flow of knowledge throughout the company, which allows Tesla to stay agile and compete against much larger car companies despite its smaller size.

McDonald's

Each year, McDonald's trains tens of thousands of new employees across its 38,000 restaurant locations worldwide. The scale of the fast-food giant's L&D programme is mind-boggling, and conventional centralized approaches to training simply aren't cut out for the job. Although the storied fast-food giant has a global L&D department, its training programmes must be tailored to the needs of individual locations, which operate across a wide variety of cultures and languages. As a result, McDonald's has leveraged several aspects of collaborative learning to empower its frontline employees to learn their jobs quickly, while also emphasizing continuous learning as the pathway to career advancement.

A great example of collaborative learning at McDonald's is its employee mentorship programme. All employees receive a basic orientation lecture as part of their onboarding process, but that's where the top-down approach to learning ends. The majority of training for new employees happens when they are partnered with senior staff at their restaurant to learn each of the 11 stations at a typical McDonald's location. Importantly, this mentorship programme continues throughout the employee's tenure at the company through McDonald's McDMentoring programme, which assigns each learner a dedicated coach to help them develop new skills and develop their leadership capacity within the company.

Here we see two principles of upskilling from within in action. First, McDonald's is leveraging its internal experts – senior employees – to teach newcomers the ropes. While the company certainly has the budget to retain dedicated training staff, it understands that the people who are best equipped to teach are the people who are actually doing the work. Second, McDonald's is emphasizing learning by doing. Rather than have employees sit in a seminar for several days and get lectured about how to do their jobs, they learn how the restaurant operates by contributing to the workflow. This is both a more efficient way of training and helps keep new employees engaged.

A key to McDonald's mentorship initiatives is its focus on building stakeholders throughout the organization. In 2011 the company launched a new training curriculum that included a module 'Leaders as teachers', which taught managers and other senior staff members how to be effective mentors for their employees. At the same time, it built the infrastructure that managers need to learn from each other through its 'Restaurant department management' curriculum, which allows managers to virtually collaborate with one another and exchange best practices. This ensures that the leaders at McDonald's are also continuously learning and improving their ability to coach and mentor their employees without the burden of structured formal training programmes.

Google

From its humble beginnings in a garage in Palo Alto, Google has grown to become the most visited site on the internet and a critical resource for anyone trying to find information online. Today, Google – or, more precisely, its parent company Alphabet – manages a network of more than 150,000 employees and has evolved from a pure search engine into a company that dabbles in a staggering array of ventures including self-driving cars, internet-connected stratospheric balloons and the life sciences. The key to Google's success has always been its unrelenting focus on the way its employees learn and share knowledge with one another, which is intimately connected with the principles of collaborative learning.

The linchpin of Google's learning initiatives is its Googler-to-Googler (g2g) programme. This is the peer-to-peer employee education network that is responsible for 80 per cent of all tracked training at the company, and consists of a network of more than 6,000 volunteers who teach classes on topics that are vital to the organization's training needs as well as topics of employee interest.[3] This is classic upskilling from within: Googlers who volunteer for the g2g programme help their colleagues in a variety of ways, including both formal classes and informal one-on-one mentorship, across a wide variety of topics. Scan the g2g schedule and you're just as likely to find seminars on kickboxing and mindfulness as an introduction to the latest machine learning technologies.[4] The blend of professional training and personal development in the g2g network was a strategic decision by the company to boost employee engagement by letting them follow their own learning interests while cultivating a true learning culture that doesn't feel like a forced HR exercise.

While Google does retain a limited number of professional trainers to teach highly specialized classes, its L&D programme is fundamentally oriented toward peer-to-peer education, which is a hallmark of successful collaborative learning initiatives. To ensure that this distributed learning culture is embraced throughout the organization, Google adopted 'learning is social' as one of its core learning philosophies while investing the time and resources to identify and cultivate experts within Google to become mentors. The logic behind the decision was simple. As one senior executive at Google put it, 'it's very unlikely that you'll ever learn faster, or better than you will from one of your fellow employees'.[5] And according to Google's own data, the programme works. It reports that the performance of its volunteer network of educators is on par with the performance of its L&D professionals who conduct training and other learning events full time.

Google has a knack for always being one step ahead of the curve, and its approach to collaborative learning is no exception. In recent years the company has heavily emphasized the importance of continuous learning for both its own employees and workers around the world. Continuous learning, as opposed to the discrete training sessions that define conventional approaches to L&D, means creating opportunities for learners to advance their knowledge in a way that is self-directed and flexible. As Google CEO Sundar Pichai put it, this requires a fundamental shift in the way we think about what it means to learn. 'Rather than thinking of education as the opening act, we need to make sure it's a constant, natural and simple act across life with lightweight, flexible courses, skills and programmes available to everyone,' Pichai wrote in a recent essay.[6] 'In the past, people were educated and learned job skills, and that was enough for a lifetime. Now, with technology changing rapidly and new job areas emerging and transforming constantly, that's no longer the case. This is crucial to making sure that everyone can find opportunities in the future workplace.'

The exciting future of upskilling from within through collaborative learning

Tesla, McDonald's and Google are just three examples of how some of the world's largest companies are upskilling from within through collaborative learning to drive innovation, accelerate product development, and train incredible numbers of employees at scale. These companies were early adopters of collaborative learning techniques, which they have refined over time to meet the evolving needs of their employees and customers. And they're hardly alone. Organizations large and small are constantly discovering new ways to leverage digital technologies to advance their learning goals.

One of the most exciting emerging technologies in the field of collaborative learning is virtual reality (VR), which allows learners to fully immerse themselves in digital worlds with their peers. VR creates a richer learning environment because it opens up the possibility of engaging in tasks or activities that may be impossible or impractical in the real world. One of the pioneers of this approach is Walmart, which launched a VR training programme for its employees in 2016.[7] Walmart's immersive training curriculum helps employees practise interacting with customers before they ever set foot on the sales floor, and is a promising first step toward a more robust collaborative learning platform in VR. Today, Walmart's core VR training materials are solo activities that facilitate self-directed learning, but it's easy to imagine future training programmes that allow many employees to interact in virtual reality. This is already being explored in some comparatively high-risk industries like nuclear power, where VR is enabling new technicians to explore a digital replica of a nuclear power plant with their supervisor, to learn about the system before they begin working on it in real life.[8]

Another promising direction in collaborative learning is the use of artificial intelligence to stimulate learners. A recent study by AI researchers at Carnegie Mellon University found that when children engaged with a learning platform that came with an AI virtual assistant that asked them questions and discussed the learning material, they had a much deeper grasp of the material than peers who didn't have access to the AI assistant.[9] This is a promising initial result that could have important implications for the use of AI in collaborative learning in professional settings. While many professional learning platforms already use AI to some degree – typically in the form of recommendation algorithms – the next generation of collaborative learning platforms will likely incorporate far more sophisticated intelligent agents. While AI will never replace human experts in a collaborative learning system, it has the potential to dramatically expand their reach. As we saw earlier in the book, organizations sometimes struggle to recruit busy experts as mentors. But with the help of an AI assistant, these experts will be able to better triage learner requests by focusing on the needs that require a human in the loop and outsourcing more repetitive tasks to the automated system. Another promising use of AI in collaborative learning is to tighten the feedback loops for content production. Collaborative learning works best when learners are able to comment on educational media to flag outdated information. But if an AI-powered collaborative learning platform has access to a company's files, it can automatically flag potentially outdated material based on changes to key documents.

Artificial intelligence and virtual reality are both incredibly exciting technologies that will shape the future of collaborative learning in ways that we can't even imagine yet. But it's important to remember that these tools are just a means to an end. A collaborative learning programme doesn't require cutting-edge technology to be successful. What's really important is that the programme reflects the learning needs of employees and is driven by peer-to-peer interactions that are facilitated by internal experts. Some day, those experts may be robots. But for now an organization's best learning resources are its own employees.

Notes

1   M Matousek. A leaked copy of Tesla's employee handbook reveals exactly how it expects workers to push boundaries and help the company succeed, Business Insider, 13 February 2020, www.businessinsider.com/leaked-tesla-employee-handbook-reveals-high-standards-for-workers-2020-2 (archived at https://perma.cc/TB62-3XES)

2   C Blakeman. An email from Elon Musk reveals why managers are always a bad idea, Inc., 30 October 2017, www.inc.com/chuck-blakeman/an-email-from-elon-musk-reveals-why-managers-are-always-a-bad-idea.html (archived at https://perma.cc/46AJ-XQQ2)

3 Re:Work. Create an employee-to-employee learning program, Re:Work with Google, nd, https://rework.withgoogle.com/guides/learning-development-employee-to-employee/steps/introduction/ (archived at https://perma.cc/NZQ4-CVD3)

4 S Kessler. Here's a Google perk any company can imitate: Employee-to-employee learning, Fast Company, 26 March 2013, www.fastcompany.com/3007369/heres-google-perk-any-company-can-imitate-employee-employee-learning (archived at https://perma.cc/7M6F-M6FE)

5 Re:Work. Create an employee-to-employee learning program, Re:Work with Google, nd, https://rework.withgoogle.com/guides/learning-development-employee-to-employee/steps/introduction/ (archived at https://perma.cc/NZQ4-CVD3)

6 S Pichai. Digital technology must empower workers, not alienate them, NBC News, 18 January 2018, www.nbcnews.com/think/opinion/digital-technology-must-empower-next-generation-workers-not-alienate-them-ncna838806 (archived at https://perma.cc/MQN5-LATL)

7 Strivr. In the footsteps of trailblazers: How Walmart embraces immersive learning, Strivr, 11 May 2021, https://www.strivr.com/customers/walmart/ (archived at https://perma.cc/4HJH-V6GP)

8 O Popov, et al. Immersive technology for training and professional development of nuclear power plants personnel, *AREdu 2021: 4th International Workshop on Augmented Reality in Education*, 2021, https://aredu.ccjournals.eu/aredu2021/ (archived at https://perma.cc/5VKL-GN8F)

9 A Aupperlee. New research shows learning is more effective when active, Carnegie Mellon School of Computer Science, 2021, www.cs.cmu.edu/news/2021/yannier_koedinger_active_learning (archived at https://perma.cc/G6L8-ULRY)

10

Convexity

How we set people free and bring collaborative learning to life at 360Learning

Throughout this book we've looked at how collaborative learning helps people everywhere upskill from within, and, more specifically, how the world's leading companies are using collaborative learning to grow together and solve impossible problems. But what about us? What's the real story with collaborative learning at 360Learning?

As I admitted up front in the introduction, collaborative learning isn't always easy to get right. To truly set people free to chart their own course and prove their impact, you need to have a few tough conversations first. How can you balance learner autonomy against leadership priorities? What does it really mean to support flexible working? And transparency sounds great in practice, but where does it stop? Is nothing secret anymore?

Unfortunately, for larger organizations with their own special kind of administrative inertia, these conversations can be even tougher. But don't worry – we've experienced these teething issues ourselves, and now we're here to help you find a way through. In this chapter we'll take you inside our culture designed to set people free, leverage internal expertise and bring collaborative learning to life: 'Convexity'. From radical transparency on salaries to getting the balance right when it comes to remote work and letting people know exactly where their careers are going from month to month, we'll show you how we've created a culture to connect people and help them focus on what's important to them.

What most organizations get wrong about culture

Most businesses build their culture with entirely the wrong goal in mind. Instead of looking for ways to support people to work the way *they* want to, they look for ways to make everything standardized, countable and predictable. This is understandable, of course – when you're growing at a rapid pace, it's only natural to prioritize predictability over innovation, or easy administration over true flexibility for employees. But this kind of prescriptive, top-down management culture – in other words, a 'because I said so' culture – doesn't just make it harder to attract the talent growing businesses need to grow and to attract more clients and customers. Counterintuitively, it actually makes it a lot *harder* to scale. That's because a rigid, top-down culture of management and leadership is only as good as the ideas, experience and talents found within the C-suite. When a work culture only encourages hierarchy and obedience, it's a lot harder for great ideas – and in a competitive market, potentially life-saving ideas – to percolate upwards and get the attention they really deserve.

Too often, organizations think about culture as a tool to make life easier for management. In this mindset, culture is just a chance to make everyone work in exactly the same way. This makes it easier to chart progress and measure impact. Or so goes the conventional wisdom. But people aren't all the same. This prescriptive culture only blinkers our thinking, limiting our ability to solve tough problems. It's also a huge waste of all the knowledge, expertise and experience people bring with them when they join us. This culture is no longer acceptable. People have had enough of being told how to work, and they've had enough of jobs that don't give them the chance to show what they can really do.

We started 360Learning with a clear vision. Our platform is built around the premise that we make the greatest impact when we connect people, give them the tools they need, get out of the way and let everyone upskill from within. So we needed a culture to do that too. That's why we built our unique culture around autonomy and accountability, called Convexity. We wanted to smash hierarchy and do-as-I-say management wherever we found it. We wanted to focus on personal responsibility at every step, and stay lean as we grew. We wanted to make it easy to leverage and celebrate our fantastic internal expertise. And now that we're growing at such a fast pace, our Convexity culture is more important than ever.

We built the 360Learning platform on the premise that learning should never be subject to anyone's approval. Instead, it should be decentralized, spontaneous and continuous. But making collaborative learning real through our Convexity culture involves one key question: how do we balance autonomy and impact?

The real challenge of balancing autonomy and impact

As Steve Jobs said, 'It doesn't make sense to hire smart people and then tell them what to do. We hire smart people so they can tell us what to do.' That's why we built a culture that gives people the opportunity to move quickly. We want our teams to be unencumbered by hierarchy, authority and process for the sake of process. We want them to have full autonomy in achieving a clearly defined set of shared goals. But this focus on autonomy is hard-earned, and comes at a cost: to balance things out and keep everyone moving in the same direction, you also need a culture of transparency, accountability and, above all else, impact.

At 360Learning everyone has access to every single piece of information they would ever need, without having to ask for it. That's why we delete information silos and make sure all information is accessible, for example by using Trello and other asynchronous tools. This way, people can define and solve problems without having to wait for others, and without worrying whether they're following the right prescriptive process. Essentially, they're free to take whatever steps they feel they need to in order to achieve their publicly documented goals and priority outcomes: their personal and team objectives and key results (OKRs). At the same time, they're accountable for achieving these OKRs, and their performance in doing so is publicly assessed each quarter down to the percentage point.

So, how do we achieve this balance of impact and autonomy, and stay nimble while we scale? The answer is: Convexity.

Our solution: Convexity

Small teams can work fast and stay lean. When we started 360Learning, we were a tiny team of around 15 people, with a strong focus on trust, impact and accountability. As we began working with more clients, it became harder for us to stay lean. We needed a way to empower every member of our team to do their best work by focusing on results over processes. We needed to scale without losing any aspect of our distinctive culture, and without creating the need for information silos, territorial management, or the kind of prescriptive and defensive learning culture we encountered in Dave's story in Chapter 5.

To achieve this goal of decentralized culture, we got specific about what makes us different, and we distilled it down to a concrete set of values: Convexity. So, what is Convexity, exactly? Convexity is our framework for maximum freedom, impact and accountability. It allows us to deliver exponential impact, implement low authority and promote a fully flexible lifestyle for individuals. Not just some flexibility – lunch breaks between 12pm and 2pm, occasional time off to attend medical appointments – but full flexibility. Within reason, our teams can work whenever, wherever and however they want – providing they meet or exceed their OKRs.

With Convexity, we divide responsibilities into subsets that are *mutually exclusive and collectively exhaustive*. We place high expectations on people to succeed, and keep everyone on track by referring to a public record of individual performance. But to make this culture real, we knew we couldn't just define it from the top. We had to make Convexity everyone's responsibility, and spread ownership among every team.

We do this through our 13 Convexity guilds, each with their own team of 360Learners charged with creating new initiatives to further this particular goal, and to find areas of improvement in existing systems and processes. These 13 guilds are:

- impact
- low authority
- rational thinking
- high accountability
- transparency
- benevolence
- hire up
- your life your way
- repeatable solutions
- personal growth
- continuous feedback
- simplicity
- prosperity

Each of these guilds encourages specific behaviours and practices designed to further our shared Convexity goals. Every new hire is encouraged to join these guilds and own our culture, and everyone takes responsibility for advancing ideas and policies to strengthen this culture. They then become the owners of these values, and are tasked with finding ways to improve our habits, processes and ways of working. We even reflect these guilds in our performance recognition system, recognizing people for their contributions to our values.

Here's how it works: let's say you're a representative of the repeatable solutions guild. During one of your onboarding sales discovery meetings, you might hear a useful nugget of information –

for example, there might be a better way for our reps to talk about the process of migrating existing learning content libraries into the 360Learning platform. It's such a useful insight that you decide to document it in Trello, ping our sales enablement coach and other individuals with a role to play in sales training and recommend it for inclusion in our sales rep onboarding modules. At this point, congratulations are in order – as a new hire, you've discovered a repeatable solution and added to our collective capabilities by capturing the knowledge to benefit others. In other words, you're helping everyone to upskill from within.

That's Convexity in practice, and it's how we make collaborative learning real. Now, time for a quick tour through the top Convexity questions – the things people can't help but ask.

We don't negotiate salaries – instead, we calculate them

Of all the questions we get about Convexity, this is the big one: how do we stay transparent on questions of salaries and remuneration? If we're so committed to openness and sunlight on all things, how do we handle paycheck questions? It all comes back to our values of low authority, simplicity and high accountability.

Like all mature organizations, we use salary ranges to structure our compensation policy. But unlike what happens in many organizations, our salary ranges aren't just a soft guideline that falls apart whenever reality comes knocking on the door: they are law. When the yearly compensation reviews come up, our salaries are calculated, not negotiated. And our laws are entirely transparent, as all laws ought to be. This is our way to stay accountable, operate with low authority and eliminate bias.

We trust 360Learners – and aspiring 360Learners – to be capable of handling important information like salary bands. That's why we practise transparency around compensation management and keep each other honest by not hiding anything. We also use the OKR system to drive performance, and we don't want our coaches to lead with the paycheck. That's why coaches aren't in charge of compensation decisions at 360Learning. This helps us live our commitment to low authority.

Our approach to salary negotiation isn't just a way to give our employees the culture they deserve – it's also selfish in a manner of speaking, because it saves managers and leaders a lot of stress, anguish and frustration. For a lot of organizations, compensation questions take up way too much time. In contrast, our compensation review this year was just one all-hands meeting during which we shared the model, as opposed to the typical dozens of alignment meetings and one-on-one discussions. Instead, we have a model that's mathematical, and we don't authorize ourselves to deviate from that. This means our salary levels aren't affected by personality biases or social inequities, such as the fact that 60 per cent of women say they never negotiate their salaries.[1] The upshot? Receiving an offer from 360Learning will be the last time a new hire has to negotiate their salary. Even then, they might feel like we're not giving them a lot of wiggle room... because we aren't.

It's all about calculating the right level. Internally, we use a factor-based method to compute levels and manage career progression for every 360Learner. We do the same with candidates, based on how we assess them against the requirements of each role, and using our current teams as comparators. As a new hire interviews with us, the interviewing team assigns them a level, which then comes into focus as they progress through the stages of the hiring process.

When we make an offer, we tell the candidate what their default level is. This level is not negotiable – we know better than that – and is visible to all other 360Learners when a new hire joins. In return, our new hires see the level of all 360Learners. In our experience, this transparency is the best way to calibrate ourselves as a collective, make the best decisions and keep everyone honest. With our levels established, we then go to our salary ranges. These ranges are designed to target the 70th percentile of the tech market, meaning we want to be within the top 30 per cent when it comes to cash compensation. We build our ranges based on market data purchased from special-ized vendors. Our salary ranges are reviewed each year so as to fully capture the market movements and our company's hypergrowth.

We have one set of salary ranges for each job market we operate in (as of writing this, France, the United States, the United Kingdom and Germany), and one salary range for each distinctive group of functions (we have eight ranges at the moment: Sales, Business Development, Sales Engineering, Client Success, AI/Machine Learning, General Tech, Support/Admin, and Default). Each of these salary ranges determines how much we offer. For example, if a person applies for an account executive role in the United States and we assess you as a senior manager 4.5, you'll be matched against the US – Sales – 4.5 range. This information is made public to every 360Learner and helps everyone to know exactly what to expect from the salary review process.

This transparency is a huge part of our Convexity culture. And, believe it or not, it's also a huge part of how we support people to learn together. By making salaries one less thing people have to worry about, they have a lot more time to focus on the things that really matter, like their own development, learning and growth.

How we demonstrate our commitment to 'your life your way'

The second big Convexity question that comes up again and again is around remote work, and how we've managed to crack the code to create a positive, nurturing team environment that gives people the flexibility and support they really need.

Due to the period of Covid-induced remote work, many employers have been persuaded of the benefits of working from home. They're reassured that its disadvantages are minimal – or at least outweighed by the benefits. In other words, they've seen the light, and are willing to embrace full remote, flexible or hybrid models, even outside pandemic conditions.

But we don't want to get complacent. We're coming off the heels of a once-in-a-century health crisis, and emotions are heady. Just because employers feel this way now doesn't mean the pendulum won't swing back the other way, as it so often does. The time was ripe for a more generous remote work policy, and the pandemic pushed the world's hand. But if we aren't careful to fully, deliberately and properly embrace what this represents – a true paradigm shift – we risk backsliding bit by bit into the pre-pandemic status quo. Companies that don't build in room for socializing – remote or otherwise – might see employee complaints about feeling isolated pile up. Similarly, leadership teams who haven't set up the proper processes to support their new remote-first policies will likely get bogged down in inefficiencies.

At 360Learning, we didn't need a lockdown to discover that our employees were just fine working from home. In fact, we'd had a remote-friendly policy in place from the very beginning. Covid-19 helped us refine an existing framework – one which we'd recommend to any organization looking to fully embrace a different and sustainable way of working. In practice, we make our commitment to 'your life your way' and flexible working real through the following practices:

- **Minimum number of meetings:** We keep synchronous meetings to a minimum, and are sure to record and share written notes to ensure full transparency. This means time zones and physical distances become much less of a barrier to efficient communication.

- **Asynchronous work:** In the same vein, we favour asynchronous work over synchronous work as much as possible. We have a robust system for using Trello as a project management and information-sharing repository, and each new hire is rigorously trained from week one on how to adapt this process.

- **Written communication:** Hand in hand with a minimum number of meetings and asynchronous work is a preference for written communication. Trello comments, Google Docs, slides... projects should be in writing and fully transparent so that everyone has equal access to information, anytime, anywhere.

- **Clear scope and high accountability:** For true asynchronous (and remote) work to flourish, each employee needs to have a clear understanding of their scope and a firm sense of accountability. Many meetings and chats are avoided when there is nothing fuzzy about who does what and who, at the end of the day, is responsible for which projects. We use the OKR system, updated each quarter and shared transparently, to keep everyone on the same page.

- **Metrics-driven environment:** How can you tell if you've succeeded in the scope you're accountable for? If the OKRs you've set for yourself, as measured by the right metrics, are achieved. Using quantifiable metrics instead of subjective indicators keeps everybody honest and on track, whether you're in the same office or 1,000 miles away.

- **Transparency and communication:** No 'water-cooler talk' or backdoor meetings. Top-down and bottom-up, communication needs to be written, but also transparent and frequent. We avoid emails, and we're sure to maintain a bi-weekly all-hands where questions submitted anonymously are answered. Salaries, performance reviews... it's all written, communicated and public.

Working from home can be extremely beneficial for the individual employee and company alike. Removing commuting time (and stress and budget) can add hours to someone's day, making them more productive, concentrated and satisfied: in short, promoting work–life balance. It also opens up recruiting possibilities to far-flung applicants and reduces the impact of differences in time zone (increasingly important as companies become more global), and it can bring different teams – but also external providers, freelancers or agencies – onto the same page. The budget that used to be spent on office expenses can now be put to better use, and nomad-minded workers can try living in a new city if they're so inclined.

What 'personal growth' looks like in reality for 360Learning engineers

Finally, let's take a look at the last big Convexity question people always ask: how does personal growth really work in specific roles? And what should 360Learners – and future 360Learners – expect from their own career growth with us?

One of the tools we use to provide transparency to our teams around professional development is our Career Path framework. A Career Path is a standardized set of skills we can use to assess performance and frame conversations around professional development. It's a tool that gives employees a clear perspective on how they can grow within 360Learning, and what exact skills they would need to develop to get there. We've been using a Career Path system since 2019, but we realized it needed tweaking: it was too complex and difficult to use in practice; it didn't reflect the value we place on soft skills; and it was too subjective.

So, in 2021, we decided to write a new engineering Career Path from scratch, using the work of companies like Spotify and Medium as inspiration. Five volunteers from our Engineering team helped to design and write the Career Path, gathering feedback from the whole team to refine it and ship it.

When revamping our Engineering Career Path, we decided to limit the grid to five core skills: technical mastery, product crafting, organizational mindset, collective improvements and community. Any more, and the assessment process would be too complex, and certain important skills wouldn't get the attention they deserve. Then, each skill is divided into six different levels, which are ordered according to the scale of impact they have (from individual impact to impact on the whole company and the market). Level one, for instance, includes skills whose impact is mostly at the individual level – an employee who follows best practices, works autonomously and demonstrates their impact at the basic level. Higher levels will reflect skills that have a more far-reaching impact.

Standardizing the skills and levels in this way allows us to unify the progress in each skill and maintain the same range of expectations for each level. In order to ascend the levels, the skills in all the previous levels need to be mastered. These levels define the expectations we have from developers in this skill, with level one being the lowest set of expectations and level six the highest.

For each level in the Career Path, we include:

- **A brief description:** This gives an overview of the expectations for this level. Here's an example from level one of technical mastery: 'Is able to develop simple features and is actively learning with the help of their peers. May infrequently have issues following patterns/ practices in existing code.'

- **A list of hard requirements:** This is a list of precise and objective behaviours or actions that are required to reach the level. All of these hard requirements must be met for a developer to reach the given level. Here is an example from level one of technical mastery: 'Always writes tests whenever it's straightforward to do so (test file already exists, or there are multiple examples to get inspired from).'

- **A list of soft requirements:** This is a list of examples of behaviours or actions expected at this level. There is no fixed rule about how many requirements are needed to validate the level, so usually we estimate someone must reach half of the soft requirements to reach the level. Some of these requirements can be a bit more subjective. Here is an example from level one of technical mastery: 'Knows when to ask for help, who to ask, and doesn't get stuck on a problem.'

This combination of hard and soft requirements allows us to have clear and equal expectations for everyone, while keeping enough flexibility to recognize specific behaviours. This Career Path grid is a cornerstone of how we coach the Engineering team, and we use it at different levels of our feedback loops: to create alignment between reviewers, to help developers see how their role can evolve, and to establish clear expectations for everyone. This is Convexity in action, and it's a big part of bringing our commitment to collaborative learning to life.

So, that's an all-too-brief overview of our Convexity culture, and how we use specific defined values to live our commitment to upskilling from within through collaborative learning. And remember, just like collaborative learning, Convexity is a living thing – we're always refining our systems and trying new things. If you're looking to build a culture that enables collaborative learning, we suggest you do too.

Note

1 CNBC. 60% of women say they've never negotiated their salary, CNBC, 31 January 2020, www.cnbc.com/2020/01/31/women-more-likely-to-change-jobs-to-get-pay-increase.html (archived at https://perma.cc/AB8N-Q36E)

11

How can we make upskilling from within through collaborative learning more than just another hot L&D trend?

DAVID JAMES
360Learning Chief Learning Officer

Collaborative learning, as a practice facilitated by smart technology, is an important step forward for L&D at this time. But it's at risk of becoming just another trend that comes and goes unless it leads to demonstrable, predictable and reliable impact.

According to Donald H Taylor's Global Sentiment Survey 2022, collaborative learning is the second-hottest trend in L&D (as rated by L&D professionals).[1] It seems to be the zeitgeist as an amalgamation of some evergreen L&D preferences: employees working together, building communities, leveraging technology and upskilling from within via user-generated content. What's there not to like?

The thing is, L&D seems addicted to the next new mode of delivery. Going back to the 1990s, e-learning was going to revolutionize L&D but has become a necessary evil at best – loved by L&D, loathed by those who have to 'click next' despite all the drag-and-drop and reveal box 'interactivity'. E-learning has been animated and made more entertaining. It's been shrunk into micro-learning and at the same time presented in huge content libraries so there's something for everyone. In the meantime, interactive video was all the rage. Remember that? We've seen the rise and fall of the 'Netflix for learning' and gamification and serious games have become L&D's attempts to get some modicum of engagement from employees, while blaming those who don't engage for not appreciating what we do – and not knowing how to learn!

When predicting the future of learning, especially tech, many wish to predict future ways that content will be filtered and consumed but this is more of the same for L&D in which new and novel modes of delivery succeed yesterday's favourites due to their predecessors' inability to exact quantifiable improvement and growth. Just check out previous years of Donald H Taylor's Global Sentiment Survey and pay your respects to the hot topics of yesteryear. May they rest in peace and not return as zombies to reclaim our attention.

We in L&D justify previous investments in learning tech with slivers of anecdata we may have collected and the unintended consequences of previous investments ('It was our first learning platform and we did get to learn about what people didn't like'). This will continue until L&D know precisely what they are trying to achieve, right down to the role and tasks – and work with people until they are actually performing the way they are expected to and delivering the results at work that they are employed for.

This cannot be done top-down in a conversation about learning needs and will not happen by chance just because there is unlimited off-the-shelf content in a platform and employees all become self-directed learners. To quote the late Geary Rummler, 'We can't get there from here,' meaning that providing more learning will not deliver better results. We have to do something different. That's our real challenge.

The real challenge: Matching employee priorities with the right learning experiences

Instead of looking for learning needs and creating learning content, we must recognize the biggest priorities for employees as they seek to assimilate and mature in the context of their work, as they transition to their next role, and for the organization to capitalize on opportunities and to mitigate risks. This is a different conversation with stakeholders.

One of the biggest shifts to pivot from 'making learning available' to 'making a predictable and meaningful impact' is to recognize that 'learning' is one way to affect the way that work is done and the results achieved by employees and that by focusing on 'performance' (the work that is to be done in the expected and rewarded ways in any given organization, department and role) L&D and the employee are both aligned to the same thing. How often have we heard over the years that 'L&D needs to align to the business'? How is it not aligned? When L&D focuses on finding the learning needs from a performance problem. That's how.

'Learning' is the bus that employees ride to get to where they want to go. It isn't the destination. You're not going to get many adults excited about going on a never-ending bus ride, but they may be motivated to take one if it takes them to where they want to go (i.e. better working and improved prospects for the future). L&D have been selling bus journeys for the sake of bus journeys – and we've spent a lot of energy trying to make those bus journeys fun. Employees have been able to see that those bus journeys are neither as fun as they're being billed, nor reliably taking them to anywhere they want to go. Going on an arduous bus ride to somewhere you might not like, when you have more pressing priorities, is not very appealing.

This doesn't mean clearing the decks and not providing learning programmes and content. I always advocate: if you know it works then keep it. But if you don't know if it works, it probably doesn't. We owe it to our organizations and our stakeholders to achieve the outcomes required.

In about 20 per cent of cases, stakeholders will ask for training and the outcome they want to achieve is that their team attended training. It's to tick a box, and they will probably be back next year for the same. For the other 80 per cent, they will ask for training but really they are asking for help and so it's our job to help them achieve the outcome they desire rather than take the order.

Alongside the right exploratory conversation about the required outcomes of our intervention and recognition of those employees who are responsible for those outcomes, we should seek data to validate to what extent it is a problem that is being experienced or a misrepresentation, which is easily and commonly done because of a limited and distorted observation of the problem, or a desire to implement 'best practices' rather than understand the pressing concerns of those doing the work. To uncover the truth, taking learning needs as assumptions that need to be validated with data by illustrating the impact of the problem is an important step in understanding, both if it is a real problem (or a misnomer as highlighted above) and to what extent it is a problem that requires intervention and a commitment to overcoming it – by all parties.

For example, we should explore data that does indeed illustrate that the way the team is currently working means it is missing service-level agreements with representatives of the team to highlight to them that things aren't working, and that they need to work together to fully understand why and what they need in order to make improvements. How different this is to consuming off-the-shelf content in the hope that it may make a difference in the unique context of a department and role.

Impactful learning isn't about providing more learning – it's about being selective

So, we seek data to validate that there is a problem and the scale of it, and we understand the problem with those responsible for the work and outcomes. The data is used to engage a representative group of those responsible for the work in a conversation about their experience, what's stopping them achieving the expected performance and results and what they need. Alongside the stakeholder who requested help in attendance, this is as likely to shed light on the situation for them as it is for us.

These conversations will never not surprise you and your stakeholders in terms of what people are experiencing and need. Much of what comes up will not be the role of L&D to solve – but then only looking for learning needs is often too small a piece of the puzzle and in isolation will make very little difference to performance if the other factors aren't addressed. This broader conversation to gain evidence via the experience of those responsible for doing the work will put everything on the table to be discussed and addressed.

The employees' role after recognizing all the important factors affecting performance and results is to prioritize those highlighted and to choose only the most impactful to address and see if it makes an important difference. These factors may relate to processes, systems, organizational structures, stakeholder expectations, communication, access to information and many other things. Only a fraction of them will be the domain of L&D, i.e. knowledge, know-how and insights.

Regardless of this, you have the key stakeholders in the room accountable for the work and the team, so these partners are either committed to trying new things to improve the data or they're not. This is very different from gathering relevant knowledge and know-how and delivering a course that may or may not lead to application of new knowledge and skills after attendance.

What is certain is that whatever comes from the conversations with those responsible for the work, so much will be addressed in a collaborative approach with internal – and maybe external – subject-matter experts. The key to this is taking specific blockers to performance and outcomes to these subject-matter experts and asking them for their help in unpacking and repackaging knowledge and know-how in the context of the organization, department, teams or roles and incorporating stakeholder expectations. The hard work in interpreting expertise is done by those with the expertise and experience rather than handing that over to those with very little, which is often the case when delivering training or providing content without enough context.

The shift to upskilling from within through collaborative learning won't happen all at once

Upskilling from within through collaborative learning is the ideal solution for so many real problems that need to be addressed to enhance performance and outcomes. This is because performance is almost always inextricably linked to culture: how things are done at the organization to meet the expectations of stakeholders, customers, clients and team members. The most efficient and predictably reliable way of affecting performance is by recognizing and understanding how things should be done, and working with those who know how to navigate the culture while getting the right things done. Collaborative learning can take the form of facilitated conversations, workshops, in-person sharing sessions, panel discussions or digital resources.

Some of these require very little investment to produce and some are more expensive. What you want to do is run inexpensive experiments to see if you can move the needle on the data quickly and then iterate and automate. Do more of what works and less of what doesn't.

Begin as close to the point of work as possible, where tasks and interactions happen, and provide guidance and support to influence what happens. The further away from the point where work interventions happen, the less predictable and more risky it becomes to influence performance and outcomes.

Once we've employed a sufficiently valuable intervention, L&D should then seek to automate as much of what works as it can with smart technology that can integrate the guidance and support required to perform and get results into the tools employees use to work, at the times that guidance and support are most needed. Again, whatever form this takes, monitor that it still gets the required results, and continue to iterate over time.

In terms of reskilling, if it can be determined how employees are expected to adapt their performance (how they do their work) and/or the outcomes of their performance, then this adaptation needs to be mapped and the relevant guidance and support implemented. This could be in the form of a workshop to kick things off and give employees an opportunity to understand, followed by a simulation to safely have a go at the new expected performance and performance support in the form of digital resources that show, guide and support the new expected actions. The whole intervention is focused on competent performance and not just *attendance* and *learning*.

This can all take a matter of days and is highly likely to deliver the required results, as opposed to big bets on top-down programmes and content that do not explore the working context enough to make a difference to the work, the results expected or the longer-term capability of the workforce.

Collaborative learning in conjunction with data and evidence-based practice is the winning formula to actual performance improvement, employee development and the reskilling crisis facing organizations and industry at large.

Note

1   D H Taylor. L&D Global Sentiment Survey 2022: The long shadow of Covid-19, DHT, 8 February 2022, https://donaldhtaylor.co.uk/insight/gss2022-results-01-general/ (archived at https://perma.cc/6689-CKQA)

12

Does the shift to upskilling from within through collaborative learning spell the end of L&D as we know it?

Throughout this book we've seen the many ways that collaborative learning tools can benefit organizations by facilitating peer-to-peer knowledge construction. It's a foundational shift away from conventional approaches to L&D that unlocks latent organizational knowledge by leveraging internal expertise, promoting employee engagement and enabling the creation of dynamic educational content. But collaborative learning doesn't occur in a vacuum. As with any tech-driven paradigm shift, it has far-reaching secondary and tertiary effects, many of which cannot be fully anticipated until the system is already up and running. When an organization embraces collaborative learning, it is not merely adding a new tool to its toolbelt. Collaborative learning fundamentally alters an organization's DNA by changing the way its employees learn, work and interact with their peers.

Unsurprisingly, perhaps, the rise of collaborative learning has put many L&D professionals on high alert. While they may recognize the incredible potential of these learning systems to advance a company's L&D goals, many of them fear that the endgame of collaborative learning is to dismantle their department and render them obsolete. Seen this way, implementing a collaborative learning platform in their organization can make L&D professionals feel like they're training their replacement. One can't blame them for being wary of the entire concept!

In this chapter I hope to assuage these fears by examining the ways that collaborative learning affects the L&D function within an organization. Far from spelling the end of L&D, upskilling from within through collaborative learning opens up an exciting new professional frontier. Will collaborative learning change the role of L&D teams? Absolutely. Yet these changes are to the benefit of both L&D teams and the employees who depend on them. In their new role, L&D professionals concentrate on identifying strategic opportunities for learning and upskilling; monitor the quality of peer-driven courses; ensure the alignment between these courses and the actual learning needs of employees; and augment the decentralized learning system through coaching and mentoring.

Technology and the changing role of L&D

Learning has always been an integral part of professional development. Prior to the Industrial Revolution, L&D was typically a one-on-one relationship between an employer and an apprentice. In the 19th century, the mechanization of many industrial jobs resulted in a profound change in the way that organizations trained their workers and facilitated learning. The new technologies of the Industrial Revolution required scalable approaches to L&D that were capable of getting large groups of employees up to speed on new processes and machines as quickly as possible. This led to the formalization of organizational L&D around the turn of the 20th century, which saw the birth of the first human resource departments and large-scale employee education programmes.

Henry Ford, who pioneered the modern concept of assembly-line production, was one of the first industrialists to recognize the acute need for new approaches to L&D and the competitive advantages these programmes created for a company. In 1913, Ford Motor Company established a proto-HR function called the Sociological

Department to train assembly-line workers in relevant skills.[1] While many detractors of L&D programmes pointed out that Ford's decision to invest in employee training could also benefit competitors if those employees chose to leave, he recognized that 'the only thing worse than training your employees and having them leave is not training them and having them stay'. And so the modern concept of organizational L&D was born.

For most of the past century, L&D departments were mostly built around formal instructional training that resembled a conventional classroom. An instructor taught workers the skills they believed were most relevant for doing their jobs, and once the instructional phase was over, they were dispatched to put their newly acquired skills into action. Although this is still the dominant paradigm for L&D programmes today, the arrival of digital technologies in the workplace during the 1980s and 1990s laid the foundation for another major shift in how organizations trained their employees.

The arrival of computers and other digital technologies in the workplace marked the beginning of a profound change in the role of L&D departments. Instead of acting solely as instructors, the role of L&D professionals began to transition toward facilitating learning and training. Computers enabled asynchronous and individually centred learning. Rather than taking a one-size-fits-all approach to L&D, digital technologies allowed for more personalized and responsive training that fits the needs of individuals within the organization.

Yet, as we saw in early chapters, the first wave of digital innovation in L&D didn't fully deliver on its promise because it was still burdened with outdated modes of thinking about how employees should learn. In many organizations, e-learning tools were just a shiny new wrapper around the same old approaches to L&D. Although the role of L&D departments was certainly changing – they now had many new administrative functions, like tracking course completion and creating new digital learning assets, in addition to their primary role as instructors – they were still mostly oriented to the needs of the organization rather than the individual employees who participated in their programmes. The result was that these new technologies had limited impact on advancing an organization's learning goals and employee engagement, despite creating a profound change in the role of L&D professionals.

When we look back at the history of organizational L&D, we can see that new technologies were a primary driver of changes in the function of this department. We can also see how new L&D processes and technologies were often dismissed by organizations that feared a disruption of the status quo. Yet we can also see that the organizations that embraced new modes of learning enabled by technology reaped outsized benefits from leaning into the changing times.

In this context, the collaborative learning movement is merely the latest evolution of L&D that is driven by new technologies and better scientific insight into how people learn. L&D has always been a highly dynamic organizational function that responds to constantly changing business objectives, technologies and employee needs. This shouldn't be surprising to anyone with experience in the profession. An L&D department that is itself incapable of learning and adapting will be entirely ineffective. The key is for L&D leaders to embrace change and proactively modify their role to leverage these new technologies to improve learning outcomes. Adapting to major change is easier said than done, and it is often stressful and fraught with challenges. L&D professionals can smooth the transition by having a holistic understanding of how a new learning paradigm will affect their workflows.

CASE STUDY

GP Strategies

GP Strategies is a leading management consulting firm that is focused on helping organizations around the world prepare their workforce for disruptive transformation. GP Strategies recognized that its clients need to offer their own customers highly customized experiences that removed friction across all touchpoints. This requires a robust learning support function that can dynamically and quickly respond to evolving customer requirements. GP Strategies understood that conventional approaches to L&D weren't well equipped to handle these new customer expectations so it shifted its approach to help clients create a learner-centric L&D strategy that was designed to handle rapid and continuous change in customer needs.

Moving from an organization-centric or content-centric L&D process to one focused on learners was a massive shift for most of GP Strategies' clients, but an important one for achieving their goals. Although many companies were understandably resistant to these changes, GP Strategies found that it was possible to ease them into the transition by keeping some aspects of their old L&D approach while relentlessly focusing on centring the learner in every engagement.

To help its clients, GP Strategies drew upon an internal resource it calls the Academy for Learning Professionals, an L&D programme that leverages a few key strategies to ensure that learners are at the centre of every interaction. The first strategy is to space learning over time. Unlike the 'one-and-done' approach to training that characterizes conventional L&D programmes, where learners receive all the information they need all at once, spaced learning allows learners to reflect upon what they've learned and interact with their peers to reinforce the information. A second key element of this strategy is a focus on micro-learning. Under a true collaborative learning paradigm, learners take responsibility for their own progress and move through educational material at their own pace. It is much easier to accomplish this when a learning programme is broken down into smaller pieces.

Other important elements of GP Strategies' approach to L&D focus on the relationship between learners. Collaborative learning is fundamentally a peer-to-peer approach to knowledge creation and this is at the heart of GP Strategies' programme. In order to engage learners, GP Strategies recognized that it was critically important to make learning social. As we saw in early chapters, people learn best from one another, so it's not enough to merely encourage spaced micro-learning. Learners need to be able to interact with one another to improve learning outcomes. Depending on the existing structure of the L&D programme, this can be easier said than done. To foster learner interactions, GP Strategies organized learning around cohorts, which encouraged learners to exchange knowledge because they had shared experiences. This strategy both encouraged learner interaction and boosted learner engagement – a true testament to the power of the learner-centric model of collaborative learning.

Collaborative learning and the new L&D department

Regardless of the industry it is in, an L&D department will always provide several key functions to an organization. First and foremost, it is dedicated to improving the capabilities and knowledge of its peers by facilitating the flow of relevant information to the right people at the right time. If L&D professionals are successful in this primary function, it will contribute to success in other key goals, such as boosting employee engagement and attracting and retaining talent. Taken together, these elements will create a strong workplace culture where learning is deeply embedded in the organization's value system.

Each element of the L&D function can be imagined as forming a layer of a pyramid, where improving employee capabilities is the base and creating a learning culture is the apex. The integrity of the structure depends on the robustness of its foundations, which means that it is impossible to create a robust learning culture without ensuring that employees are learning relevant skills in ways that make them want to stick around and participate to the fullest extent in the organization. As such, it is important to identify the key indicators of a vigorous L&D function and how implementing new technologies and processes may affect these indicators.

A recent report on L&D departments identified several dimensions of a strong organizational learning function based on extensive interviews with professionals in the field.[2] It's worth highlighting a few of the key dimensions and how collaborative learning will affect their implementation and outcomes.

Alignment with business strategy

The importance of aligning an organization's L&D function with its wider business strategy may seem so obvious that it doesn't even warrant mentioning. But 60 per cent of companies report that their learning strategy has little or no connection to their overall business strategy.[3]

This striking disconnect is a result of top-down L&D programmes and the technologies that are used to implement them. When learning objectives are decided by a handful of individuals at the top of an organization, there is a very good chance that those programmes won't reflect the actual needs of employees who ultimately determine business success. Although L&D leaders are typically aware of the organization's business strategy and attempt to build learning programmes to advance those goals, these programmes may still fail to deliver the right knowledge to the right people at the right time. These challenges are only exacerbated by outdated learning management systems where it takes months to develop learning materials. By the time those learning materials are distributed to employees, the strategy and goals of an organization may have changed and the learning solution is now mismatched to the problem.

When L&D teams embrace collaborative learning, they can avoid misalignment with an organization's overall business strategy because the L&D goals are organically determined in a bottom-up manner. In a collaborative learning system, employees play a significant part in determining their own learning needs and work together to create useful content that is relevant to their work. Each employee in an organization has specific, narrowly defined goals that contribute to the successful implementation of a business strategy in aggregate. By ensuring that each employee is able to meet their own learning goals, collaborative learning guarantees that L&D programmes are always aligned with the overall business strategy.

Integration across an organization

A key feature of a robust L&D programme is its integration across an organization. The best L&D programmes are structured to rapidly respond to emerging business needs, whether that is getting new employees up to speed or launching a new product or instruction on how to use a new tool or technology. In this context, a major challenge for L&D departments is triaging the needs of various departments and executives when each stakeholder wants to prioritize their learning needs. Conventional, centralized approaches to L&D are ill equipped to handle this problem. They lack robust feedback mechanisms that can identify emerging learning needs before they've become a problem or identify remaining gaps after a learning programme has been implemented. This feedback must travel up and down a chain of command within the organization, which creates delays that hobble an organization's ability to respond to a rapidly changing environment.

As we saw in Chapter 7, collaborative learning is crucial for driving success at every point in an employee's journey, from onboarding to promotion. By leveraging peer-to-peer knowledge transmission, collaborative learning ensures that all members of an organization – regardless of seniority or tenure – have their learning needs met as they arise. The ability to triage learning needs is an inherent feature of this system and occurs automatically. The result is that organizations are able to stay nimble and quickly respond to changing situations.

Insight into learning gaps

The linchpin of an effective L&D department is its insight into learning gaps across an organization. This is ultimately what informs the educational content it creates and how it is delivered to employees. Historically, identifying learning gaps in an organization has been a top-down process dictated by leadership. The problems with this approach are that it fails to address the learning needs of individuals across an organization, and it often misses learning gaps that aren't visible to executives and L&D leaders. It is implemented as though everyone in a particular cohort is at the same point in their learning journey. While it can be effective in certain contexts – such as the adoption of a new technology across the company – in most cases it falls short of addressing true learning gaps in a timely manner.

When an L&D team adopts a collaborative learning model, it removes the guesswork from identifying learning gaps. Collaborative learning systems are driven by individuals who express their learning needs and work with their peers to construct knowledge that addresses these needs. In this sense, collaborative learning is designed to automatically identify and fill learning gaps.

Design of the learning experience

With the rise of e-learning, the role of L&D departments shifted from a somewhat instructional role that centred on in-person training sessions to one that also required creating educational content that could be delivered on a learning platform. While this process did enable some degree of asynchronous learning, it lacked the ability to dynamically respond to evolving learning needs. L&D departments designed the learning experience in advance according to a multi-year organizational roadmap and released new content on a predetermined schedule.

The problem with this approach is that it effectively meant designing a learning experience for a typical employee journey that mapped to the company's idea of what that employee needed to learn. Of course, the 'average' employee doesn't exist any more than the 'average' family with 2.5 kids exists. Instead, it is an idealized abstraction of the organization's employees, which means that often this carefully crafted learning experience fails to meet the actual learning needs of employees. This is a direct consequence of many of the e-learning tools that have been embraced by L&D departments over the past decade. The slow and cumbersome process of creating education content for these platforms required planning for learning needs months in advance. In other words, it required L&D teams to predict the needs of learners rather than respond to them. The result is that by the time L&D teams release the content to learners within their organization, it is often outdated or irrelevant to their needs.

Collaborative learning platforms, by contrast, are built to enable learners to design their own learning experience. Content is created on an ad hoc basis in house by leveraging experts and peer knowledge. This profound shift is analogous to the transition to just-in-time or 'lean' processes in manufacturing. Rather than over-producing goods and racing to hit sales quotas, manufacturers were able to eliminate waste while meeting customer demand by manufacturing goods based on customer demand. Instead of pushing goods onto the market, the market pulled the goods out of manufacturers. Collaborative learning, by extension, is a 'lean' approach to knowledge production where educational materials are pulled from the organization rather than pushed upon it. Just like lean manufacturing, this eliminates wasted efforts by L&D teams while ensuring that the demand for educational content from learners is satisfied just in time.

Measuring impact

One of the most important developments of the e-learning revolution was its increased capacity to measure the engagement with L&D initiatives. Digital tools are capable of tracking an arbitrary number of learning metrics at scale, which provides quantifiable feedback to L&D professionals on their learning programmes. Yet, as many organizations have discovered, using these metrics to enhance learning outcomes is not straightforward. The reason for this is that, despite an increased capacity to measure impact with digital tools, the items that are being measured are not necessarily indicative of successful learning. For example, most L&D programmes focus on high-level metrics like course completion. While this can be a proxy for the impact of a learning initiative across an entire organization, it provides limited insight into the effectiveness of L&D programmes at the level of individual learners.

Collaborative learning platforms offer L&D teams a more fine-grained method for analysing the impact of a learning initiative. These tools allow for sophisticated impact measurements that focus on the outcomes of learning initiatives, such as their effects on individual performance, engagement, team collaboration and workflow processes. This is because collaborative learning tools create opportunities for individual learners to provide feedback on specific elements of courses through features like commenting systems while simultaneously allowing L&D professionals to track metrics like the daily engagement with the learning platform, course creation and interactions with peers.

Informal/continuous learning

A hallmark of conventional approaches to L&D is that they have focused on formal and discrete approaches to knowledge transmission. This typically takes the form of in-person training sessions or digital courses that are required at well-defined points within an employee's journey, such as onboarding or promotion. L&D departments have adopted this formalized structure of learning not because it is necessarily the best or most effective way to learn, but due to the limitations of their tools. The challenge with this approach is that it often fails to deliver instruction when the learner needs it. Instead, learning needs are determined in advance on a predetermined schedule, which means important information may be delivered too early or too late to be of much use to the learner. The result is low engagement and lacklustre improvement in learning outcomes.

Collaborative learning turns the conventional approach to L&D on its head by emphasizing continuous and informal learning. These platforms allow learners to solicit information as they need it, which fosters informal teaching opportunities. This is where the social aspects of collaborative learning platforms really shine. By creating a space for learners to interact with one another in a self-directed manner, they leverage our innate tendency to learn from our peers without the need to broadcast a learning request up a centralized chain of command. This creates an environment where continuous learning is the norm, which is the foundation of an organizational culture built around learning.

The new L&D department

Now that we've seen the various dimensions that define a strong L&D function and how collaborative learning changes those dimensions, we can return to the question at the heart of this chapter: does collaborative learning spell the end of L&D as we know it?

The answer is an unequivocal 'no'. L&D professionals still have a central and important role to play in organizations that have embraced a collaborative learning model. However, the role that the L&D department plays in the organization will change dramatically. The biggest difference is the shift from a style of top-down learning management to something that more closely resembles an L&D consultant. Under this new paradigm, L&D leaders work closely with organizational leadership as a strategic partner to help ensure that learning initiatives align with the broader business goals of the organization. As such, the key focus areas of the new L&D department will include the following.

FIGURE 12.1   Key focus areas of a new L&D department

1. STRATEGIC PARTNER   2. BUSINESS ALIGNMENT   3. COACHING AND MENTORING   4. QUALITY ASSURANCE

1 **Becoming a strategic partner to recognize and analyse needs:** Collaborative learning platforms leverage internal expertise to create performance-focused materials that meet the needs of individual learners. This reduces the amount of time that L&D professionals need to spend creating course material and gives them more time to focus on identifying strategic opportunities for collective learning based on their cultural and contextual understanding of individual learners and the overarching goals of the business. Collaborative learning platforms give them the insight

they need to identify common challenges and learning gaps across the organization so they can develop high-impact programmes that can meet the real needs of many learners.

2 **Ensuring alignment between actual business needs and L&D solutions:** A collaborative learning organization isn't created overnight. It takes time to build stakeholders and build familiarity with this new approach to L&D: upskilling from within. A frequent challenge in collaborative learning is harnessing internal expertise to meet learning needs expressed by employees. While some experts may be naturally inclined to create course materials to help their peers, others may be more reluctant to contribute or feel that they're not capable of teaching others. This challenge is particularly acute during the early days of implementing collaborative learning in an organization, and L&D professionals have an important role to play in encouraging contributions from internal experts. This ensures alignment between learner needs and course creation, which is key to an effective collaborative learning system.

3 **Coaching and mentoring:** One of the most important changes that collaborative learning brings to organizations is that it transforms L&D professionals into coaches and mentors. Indeed, these new roles are crucial to the successful creation of a collaborative learning culture. While individual learners and experts are the engine that drives the learning process, there will still be learning gaps that need to be addressed. The insights that collaborative learning platforms provide on the progress of individual learners allows L&D professionals to launch targeted interventions and significantly improve learning outcomes by acting as a coach or mentor. This has the added benefit of personalizing the learning process and improving learner engagement. Instead of feeling like a number in an organization's L&D programme, employees will see that L&D initiatives are designed to help them succeed as an individual.

4 **Quality assurance of learning materials:** Collaborative learning platforms depend on individual learners to voice their needs and internal experts to create learning materials that meet those needs.

This decentralized approach to knowledge creation and transmission has many benefits in terms of efficiency and matching resources to real needs. But it is most effective when the learning materials that are created are held to a high standard. Under the collaborative learning model, L&D professionals help shape curricula by monitoring the quality of learning materials being produced across the organization.

While these characteristics of a new L&D department are key to the successful implementation of the collaborative learning model, this is hardly an exhaustive list of the new roles and responsibilities that this system entails. The exact form that a collaborative learning L&D department takes will vary from organization to organization. But it is absolutely critical for all L&D professionals to understand that collaborative learning will require them to reorient themselves to deliver learning experiences in a different way. This process may be challenging and feel unnatural at first. Breaking old habits is hard, but embracing this new approach to learning will have a massive positive impact on improving learning outcomes in an organization.

CASE STUDY
Slack

Slack is a communications platform that is used around the world by startups and titans of industry alike. As its workforce has grown, so has the company's need to keep all of its employees on the same page even when they're thousands of miles and several time zones apart. This is a particularly important challenge to address when it comes to new hires. One of an L&D team's most important jobs is integrating new employees into the company with learning materials that allow them not only to do their job effectively, but also to get to know the company culture and their peers.

As workplaces like Slack increasingly adopt hybrid or fully remote working arrangements, they have encouraged their L&D teams to reconsider conventional approaches to onboarding new employees. The old model of gathering people in person for a few days of intensive training is no longer viable for many companies, but replicating this experience in a digital-first environment meant that Slack had to fundamentally rethink its approach to L&D in this context.

Slack's L&D team realized that a core feature of successful onboarding programmes is fostering a sense of community and helping new employees build relationships with their peers. They prioritized a strategy where the new employees – the learners – worked together rather than passively receiving information from L&D leadership. After a few community-based sessions to help new hires learn the company culture, familiarize themselves with important internal tools and meet some of their colleagues, the Slack L&D team transitions them to a self-paced content track where new hires can learn on their own schedule. In this way, they've embraced two key facets of a successful collaborative learning programme – social learning and continuous micro-learning – to successfully onboard new users.

Importantly, Slack has implemented a system for measuring the results of its new approach to onboarding. New hires are given a survey about their experience that Slack's L&D team can analyse to see what is working and areas for improvement. After making this transition to a remote onboarding process that featured many aspects of collaborative learning, the survey results showed that there were no drops in scores along key metrics like engagement, belonging and development. Although Slack's L&D team had radically transformed its onboarding process to meet the needs of an increasingly remote workforce, its decision to adopt collaborative learning practices meant that this transformation didn't result in a decline in learning outcomes.

Conclusion

To make the most of upskilling from within through collaborative learning, L&D professionals need to adapt to a radically different way of delivering learning experiences. But, as we saw in this chapter, this new paradigm isn't a death knell for L&D departments. Instead, it is the next evolution for a business function that has always ridden the waves of technological advances and used new tools to improve learning outcomes. Collaborative learning platforms allow L&D professionals to focus on their core strengths, like matching learning initiatives with business strategy, mentoring learners and stewarding organizational knowledge. It accomplishes this feat by reducing the amount of time that L&D teams need to spend on low-impact tasks like administration, increasing insight into the learning outcomes of individuals and creating new opportunities to measure impact.

This last point is especially important when it comes to implementing collaborative learning processes in an organization. L&D teams must focus on proving their impact and demonstrating the return on investment (ROI) of every learning moment as the learning process becomes more continuous and discrete. This requires new modes of thinking about how internal processes affect learning as well as new techniques for measuring learning outcomes. We'll consider these issues in more depth in the next chapter.

Notes

1 The Henry Ford. Ford Motor Company Sociological Department and English School, The Henry Ford, nd, www.thehenryford.org/collections-and-research/digital-resources/popular-topics/sociological-department (archived at https://perma.cc/66BP-6HCR)
2 J Brassey, L Christensen and N van Dam. The essential components of a successful L&D strategy, McKinsey & Company, 13 February 2019, www.mckinsey.com/business-functions/people-and-organizational-performance/our-insights/the-essential-components-of-a-successful-l-and-d-strategy (archived at https://perma.cc/8GAB-VWSC)
3 J Brassey, L Christensen and N van Dam. The essential components of a successful L&D strategy, McKinsey & Company, 13 February 2019, www.mckinsey.com/business-functions/people-and-organizational-performance/our-insights/the-essential-components-of-a-successful-l-and-d-strategy (archived at https://perma.cc/8GAB-VWSC)

13

How collaborative learning helps prove learning impact

In the past, L&D programmes may have been taken for granted and accepted as the cost of doing business. There was comparatively little regard for how those programmes were structured or their impact on the organization. If employees attended training programmes, executives assumed they were learning – and applying – newfound skills in their job.

How things have changed.

Now more than ever, L&D teams are under pressure to prove the ROI of training and skill development programmes. Executives expect L&D teams to justify every dollar they're spending and link this investment to business outcomes. It's not enough to show that employees learned a new skill or boosted sales after training. L&D teams need to demonstrate how those new skills are impacting the organization's bottom line and prove that the training is what led to an increase in sales.

The new demands on L&D teams are a result of their acceptance as a truly strategic business partner. Instead of viewing L&D as some backwater HR function, executives increasingly recognize just how important effective training is to their organization. But the elevation of L&D's status within the modern organization comes with strings attached in the sense that these teams must demonstrate that they can predictably and reliably produce results that align with business objectives.

A recent survey of L&D programmes revealed a wide gulf between how executive leaders and L&D professionals think about the results of training programmes. In response to the question 'What are the top challenges for the talent development team?', 32 per cent of executives responded with 'Demonstrating ROI' compared with only 22 per cent of people managers. This was one of the largest gaps between the respondent groups in the survey and ranked as one of the biggest challenges by executives.[1]

The lesson from these results is clear. The C-suite isn't satisfied with the ability of its L&D professionals to demonstrate the ROI of training programmes and it's critical that L&D teams find ways to prove the value that they bring to the company. The old myth that employees who have completed a training have learned valuable skills that they will apply in their day-to-day job is crumbling away. L&D teams need new ways of demonstrating the effectiveness of their programmes – and upskilling from within through collaborative learning has a lot to offer.

The old L&D measurement paradigm

The conventional method for measuring L&D outcomes focused on a few core metrics that have proven to be inadequate proxies for demonstrating the impact of these programmes. These metrics were typically centred on attendance, course completion and learner satisfaction, but they offered little insight into whether employees actually learned anything of value or applied this learning to their work. Instead, these metrics are best suited for refining the content of the learning programme itself. The problem, of course, is that this system of measurement optimizes L&D programmes for the wrong results. L&D teams could improve training sessions to boost completion and satisfaction rates without moving the needle in terms of business outcomes.

The shortcomings of the old measurement paradigm didn't result from the ignorance of L&D teams. These professionals have always been focused on boosting metrics like employee engagement and retention that are directly linked to strategic business objectives. Rather, the limitations of the measurement system were a natural result of the limitations of the conventional top-down approaches to training programmes. The simple fact is that there is no way to measure the true effectiveness of L&D programmes if they are focused on topics rather than learners. This approach erases the context in which the learning occurs, which obscures skills gaps and makes it challenging to apply learning in real-world situations.

Data suggests that only 5 to 15 per cent of people can learn out of context and then subsequently apply that knowledge to appropriate contexts.[2] This helps explain why the old approach to measuring L&D outcomes consistently fell short of its goals. A topic-centred training model is designed to measure engagement with the material rather than the impact of the training, such as improved skills, new capabilities or solving problems that couldn't have been solved before. By contrast, learner-centric approaches to L&D such as collaborative learning are designed to focus on the outcomes of training rather than the training itself. By focusing on the learner, collaborative learning ensures that new knowledge is always contextual, which allows the learner to implement it in ways that drive desired results for the organization. This is the key promise of upskilling from within.

From engagement to impact

Measuring impact is one of the thorniest challenges faced by L&D departments. If L&D professionals are unable to prove that their efforts are solving key business problems, it's difficult for them to make the case that these programmes are a worthwhile use of limited organizational resources. Today, executives expect that employees who complete training programmes will use their newly acquired knowledge to do their jobs better and help the business achieve its objectives. But before an L&D team can transition to a new training paradigm that is focused on impact, it must understand what constitutes a successful programme.

A recent survey of L&D professionals and business executives offers some instructive clues on what matters when it comes to gauging the impact of an L&D initiative.[3] The survey asked people managers and executives to name the metrics that would show the success of an L&D programme; the differences in their answers are illuminating. For example, while 65 per cent of executives cited an 'increase in performance metrics' as a hallmark of successful L&D, only 54 per cent of people managers agreed. On the other hand, 43 per cent of people managers cited 'use of learning programmes' as a mark of success compared with only 35 per cent of executives. These results illustrate the divide between executives and L&D professionals when it comes to benchmarking the effectiveness of training programmes – L&D teams are focused on engagement with the programme and executives are focused on business outcomes.

Interestingly, executives and people managers had similar scores when it came to the 'ability to apply learning' as an indicator of a successful L&D programme. This underscores the importance of shifting toward a learner-centric training model where L&D programmes are designed to solve the real problems of the people who are participating in them. The goal is to help people do what they're already doing better; and an L&D programme that has a massive library of generic content is always going to fall short of achieving this goal. The best these programmes can hope for is boosting attendance and employee satisfaction with training. Achieving meaningful results that impact business outcomes ultimately means changing what and how we measure. It requires L&D teams to stop counting hours spent in a training programme and start focusing on ways to link those hours to real-world impact.

Understanding the problem

The key to any effective system of measurement is to ensure that it is measuring the right thing. You can make a measurement system infinitely precise, but if it's measuring the wrong variables it will never produce data that can be used to achieve desired outcomes.

Digital advertising provides us with an instructive example of the perils of poorly calibrated measurement systems. As the retail magnate John Wanamaker famously quipped, 'Half my advertising spend is wasted; the trouble is, I don't know which half.' Wanamaker knew that advertising was important for driving customers into his department stores, but he lacked a measurement system that could tell him which ads were actually effective. This was a problem that digital advertising on platforms like Google and Facebook was meant to fix. These platforms have unprecedented insights into their users and can track how they engage with advertisements and which ads actually result in the customer completing a purchase. It's the kind of customer data that Wanamaker could only dream about and should, in principle, increase the effectiveness of an ad while reducing wasted marketing expenditures.

Digital ads offer a compelling story, but time and time again businesses find out the hard way that it's too good to be true. Consider the e-commerce giant eBay, which for years ran a sophisticated digital advertising programme designed to drive customers to its website. eBay paid millions of dollars per year on digital ads that would show up at the top of Google search results for queries like 'used TV eBay.' The idea was to beat out competing resellers with branded search terms that would lead people to eBay's marketplace. And for all intents and purposes, the data appeared to show that the strategy was working. People were clicking on the targeted digital ads and buying products on eBay's site.

But what was *actually* being measured here? Sure, consumers were clicking on eBay's paid advertising and buying products, yet no one could say whether they would have ended up on eBay anyway even if there wasn't a paid advertisement. About a decade ago, several economists teamed up with eBay's marketing team to get to the bottom of the question. They turned off paid advertising for several targeted search queries and waited to see the results. If eBay's ads were as effective as the data suggested, they should have seen a sharp drop off in the number of customers who were buying these products after searching for them. Instead, what they found was the exact opposite.

Turning off the paid advertising had no appreciable effect on consumer behaviour.[4]

The lesson from eBay's experience with digital advertising is that it is absolutely critical to understand the problem you're trying to solve before you implement a measuring system to track the results. The problem eBay was trying to solve was customers buying products from competing resellers instead of eBay. Their solution was targeted ads and the company thought that the data from these ads showed that they were siphoning customers away from competitors. But, as the experiment revealed, eBay's data only showed that customers who were already thinking about buying from eBay were clicking on the ad.

eBay's miscalibrated measurement system is analogous to the challenges faced by many L&D teams today. If employees attend a training session and report high satisfaction, and the business reports better sales the next quarter, it's tempting to attribute that improvement to the training. But who's to say that the increase in sales wouldn't have happened anyway even if the training never occurred? The problem is that this L&D paradigm equates employee engagement in training sessions with business outcomes, yet there is little to no evidence to substantiate this link. As we saw earlier, this is not because L&D teams don't want this information. It's because until recently they lacked the tools that can rigorously connect L&D initiatives with business outcomes.

For L&D teams, understanding the problem means understanding learner needs. In the past, L&D teams made educated assumptions about learner needs based on limited employee feedback and directives from the C-suite. All too often, however, these assumptions were not based in the lived reality of employees. The result was an explosion of generic content on learning platforms that met the needs of no one in particular. L&D teams could count employee course completion and distribute surveys to measure satisfaction, and if these happened to align with business outcomes they could pat themselves on the back and call it a win.

This strategy is rapidly becoming obsolete as executives demand more robust evidence that L&D programmes are contributing to strategic objectives. The only way to demonstrate the true impact of a training programme is to ensure that it is addressing real problems within the organization. This means that L&D professionals can no longer make assumptions about employee learning needs or even take professed learning needs at face value. Instead, they need to find the data that indicates that these learning needs represent real problems.

What this means in practice is engaging with stakeholders throughout the organization to identify gaps between desired performance and results, and the causes of these deficits. If an employee or team requests training on a particular subject, it is important for the L&D team to work with those stakeholders to understand why this is a problem now and the desired performance outcomes of implementing the training. This is a profound shift from the old way of doing things, which would focus on learning objectives. Aside from ensuring that L&D programmes are working to solve actual problems, a further upshot of this approach is that it increases the L&D team's credibility by focusing on outcomes that are important to *the stakeholders* rather than the L&D team.

How to measure what matters

Once an L&D team has confidence that it has identified real problems within an organization that require training or other learning initiatives, it can begin triaging these problems and help stakeholders develop performance-oriented materials tailored to learning needs. This will give the L&D teams confidence that their programmes are effective, but they still need a method for measuring the impact on business outcomes.

All training evaluation models are meant to provide frameworks for analysing the effectiveness of learning programmes by answering key questions like what was learned, whether the learning was successful, whether employees use the new knowledge on the job and how training can be improved. Many of the most popular training evaluation models that are capable of linking learning programmes with business impact have been under development for decades and come with trade-offs that are important to understand for any L&D team. In this chapter we'll consider three of the leading techniques for evaluating the business outcomes of learning programmes, and how they can be implemented to maximize impact.

The Kirkpatrick model

Don Kirkpatrick was a professor emeritus at the University of Wisconsin and a former president of the American Society for Training and Development who is best known for the training evaluation model that bears his name. Originally developed in 1959 in a series of articles published in the *Journal of the ASTD*, the Kirkpatrick model rose to prominence with the publication of *Evaluating Training Programs* in the early 1990s. Today, the Kirkpatrick model is easily the most widely used method for evaluating learning programmes and is valued for its ability to connect quantifiable metrics like sales or retention to skills learned during training.

The Kirkpatrick model consists of four tiers that are meant to be evaluated in a serial manner: Reaction, Learning, Behaviour and, finally, Results. At the first level, L&D teams should gauge the reactions of employees immediately after training. This can be accomplished through surveys that are designed to elicit information about how employees felt about the training, such as whether they found the information useful and if the information was presented clearly. This is a technique that is likely already familiar to many L&D teams as it provides the basis for measuring engagement in conventional training programmes.

The next tier requires L&D teams to assess whether employees retained the knowledge they received during training. This can involve formal tests or assignments that require the employees to implement their new knowledge. Depending on the structure of a training programme, these techniques may already be used by many L&D teams.

The third tier of the Kirkpatrick model is where many L&D professionals struggle. This level is meant to assess behavioural changes in employees in order to understand whether they are using their new skills on the job. There are many different techniques for accomplishing this, including spot inspections, manager evaluations or even self-assessments. The reason why many L&D teams fail to implement this process is because it requires significantly more effort to obtain the relevant data. It requires working closely with individual employees, monitoring entire teams, and open lines of communication with managers who are best positioned to see changes in employee behaviour.

The final tier of the Kirkpatrick model is measuring results. This means looking at the effects of training programmes on the overall performance of a company along key metrics such as improved sales, higher retention rates or increased levels of production. Although the Kirkpatrick model is designed to work from tier 1 to tier 4, successfully implementing this type of training evaluation requires L&D teams to start by identifying the results they want to achieve and then working backwards. Since each tier in the model is meant to serve as the foundation for analysis at higher levels, it is critical that L&D professionals don't wait to start measuring results until the fourth tier. They must collect and analyse relevant data at each step in the learning journey so they can synthesize this information and get an accurate understanding of how a given training programme impacts business outcomes.

The Kirkpatrick model of training evaluation has been incredibly successful at helping organizations link learning programmes with strategic business objectives. Despite its popularity, however, it is not without shortcomings. One of the biggest oversights of the Kirkpatrick model is that it fails to provide a cost–benefit analysis that shows the true ROI of a training programme. It provides quantifiable results of the programme, but it doesn't reveal whether these results outweigh the costs of the training.

The Phillips model

The model developed by Jack Phillips was meant to solve the shortcomings of the Kirkpatrick model and provide a solid basis for demonstrating the ROI of a learning programme. It was first outlined in Phillips' 1980 book, *Return on Investment in Training and Performance*, and has seen widespread adoption as business leaders began to demand demonstrable ROI on their L&D function.

The Phillips model shares many features with the Kirkpatrick model, with a few key differences. It is divided into five tiers, with the fifth and final tier devoted to quantifying the ROI of a training process. The first two levels – Reaction and Learning – are borrowed almost unchanged from Kirkpatrick. In the third level, Phillips departs from the Kirkpatrick model's notion of Behaviour, which he changed to Application and Implementation. Unlike Kirkpatrick, Phillips didn't think it was sufficient to simply identify changes in employee behaviour as evidence of the effectiveness of a learning programme. Instead, he also requires L&D teams to look for factors outside the training process that may help or hinder the impact of the training, such as the adoption of new tools or internal processes. This adds more context to the learning programme that can help trainers identify whether problems are endogenous to the training programme or are the result of changes outside of the L&D team's purview.

Like Kirkpatrick, Phillips devoted the fourth tier of his training evaluation model to measuring Impact (referred to as 'Results' under the Kirkpatrick model). Phillips' key point of departure at this tier is that his system takes into account both positive and negative impacts of a training programme. This gives a more holistic picture of the impact of the learning initiative and helps trainers identify areas for improvement that can have a significant effect on business outcomes.

The biggest change in Phillips' model is the introduction of a fifth tier meant to explicitly measure the ROI of an L&D programme. This involves synthesizing data from the previous four tiers to perform a cost–benefit analysis. The basic idea here is to translate quantifiable impact metrics from lower tiers and convert them into dollar values. This allows executives to determine whether a given training programme is worth the resources the company is devoting to it. Calculating the ROI of a training programme requires L&D teams to consider a number of factors, such as resource development costs (how much it costs to implement the course, including the price of the L&D platform being used and the cost of developing content for the platform), time costs (derived by multiplying the number of hours employees spend on the programme and the hourly cost of each employee) and implementation costs (such as technical support or rental space).

Brinkerhoff Success Case Method

The Brinkerhoff Success Case Method is a more recent training evaluation method that is notable for its departure from purely quantitative metrics for measuring the impact of learning programmes. Developed by Robert Brinkerhoff in 2003, the Success Case Method is designed to help an organization understand why a training programme is or is not working based on qualitative evidence.

Unlike the Phillips model, the Brinkerhoff approach doesn't attempt to calculate a monetary value for training outcomes to derive a cost–benefit analysis. Instead, it focuses on cultivating examples of a learning programme's impact that can be used to demonstrate the value of the initiative to executives and other stakeholders. The model focuses on learning outcomes, which means there is no guesswork involved in isolating the variables that are used as input to statistically demonstrate the link between a learning programme and its impact on an organization. The goal is to produce compelling case studies that show how a learning programme is successful, while simultaneously identifying areas for improvement.

The Brinkerhoff Success Case Method is divided into four steps. The first step is to identify training goals and expectations. The idea is to rigorously define the outcomes that would mark the training programme as a success. This can take many different forms, such as boosting production or reducing sales cycle time. The important thing is to make sure that these desired results are explicitly defined.

The next step is to identify the outliers in a given learning programme. This means finding the learners who had the best results *and* those who had the worst results. This can be accomplished through a survey or through quantifiable metrics like the number of hours an employee spends on a relevant task.

The third step involves studying the outliers in greater detail through in-depth interviews, spot observations or other methods. The goal is to understand how the training programme enabled some employees to flourish while other employees floundered. This allows L&D teams to refine training to drive better outcomes for all participants.

In the final step, L&D professionals synthesize the information they have gathered to create case studies and reports outlining how the training programme translated into results. The case studies should focus on the success stories and highlight how the learning initiative empowered employees to overcome obstacles that might otherwise have been impossible or to identify opportunities using their new knowledge. The reports, on the other hand, should also identify areas for improvement based on the experience of employees whose training didn't improve results for the company.

Collaborative learning and measuring ROI

The training evaluation models outlined above are just a few of the frameworks available to L&D teams to measure the impact of their learning programmes. There are many other methods worth exploring, such as the CIRO, Kaufman or Anderson models, and each has its own trade-offs. I wanted to focus on the Kirkpatrick, Phillips and Brinkerhoff models because they are the most widely used and, in my opinion, the best positioned to demonstrate the ROI of L&D programmes. Ultimately, however, L&D teams need to select a learning evaluation model based on the unique needs of their organization.

Regardless of the specific measurement system chosen, the important thing is that L&D teams ensure that they are enabling meaningful measurement in every learning experience. Old approaches to L&D were poorly equipped to handle this level of measurement, and this is a primary reason why so many L&D programmes have struggled to improve business outcomes through training programmes. It doesn't matter how much content is produced or how high attendance and satisfaction scores are – if L&D teams aren't measuring the right things, they'll never be able to prove the ROI of training programmes.

In this respect, collaborative learning platforms are unparalleled in their ability to link learning programmes to business impacts. The reason why collaborative learning platforms are so good at measuring impact is because they are inherently learner focused. Unlike systems that are content-centric, collaborative learning systems are designed to create knowledge through peer-to-peer interactions and come with built-in feedback mechanisms. This ensures that knowledge is always contextualized and addressed to the real needs of learners. It removes guesswork for the L&D team in terms of identifying real problems because these problems are voiced organically by users as they experience them.

Importantly, collaborative learning systems are also built to collect relevant data across various scales, including individuals, teams and the entire organization. Unlike previous learning platforms that were limited to measuring course completion and user satisfaction, collaborative learning tools can track important metrics, such as whether learners are applying what they've learned. This can be tracked by integrating collaborative learning platforms with other digital tools that are explicitly linked to business objectives, such as customer relationship management software, which allows L&D teams to rigorously quantify how a training impacts performance metrics like the number of sales or the number of service tickets completed.

Finally, collaborative learning platforms are designed to significantly boost the ROI of training programmes by removing costly elements of implementing training. Previous approaches to L&D have involved creating expensive training materials, renting equipment and space, and may have required employees to sacrifice large blocks of time to attend training sessions. Collaborative learning avoids these costly factors by leveraging internal expertise and peer-created content while fostering continuous learning that allows employees to engage with training materials in micro-lessons. Together, these features drive down the cost of L&D programmes, which increases the likelihood that they generate a positive ROI for the company.

Now that we've seen how collaborative learning tools help L&D professionals prove the impact of learning initiatives, we're ready to look at some examples in practice. In the next chapter we'll examine how companies in industries like healthcare, manufacturing and business-to-business software are upskilling from within through collaborative learning to help with everything from building the right employee skills to preparing an ageing workforce for the technologies of tomorrow.

Notes

1 LinkedIn. LinkedIn workplace learning report, LinkedIn, 2018, https://learning.linkedin.com/content/dam/me/learning/en-us/pdfs/linkedin-learning-workplace-learning-report-2018.pdf (archived at https://perma.cc/HC68-H5GZ)

2 D James. The pivot from 'learning' to 'performance': An expert interview with Guy Wallace, 360Learning, nd, https://360learning.com/blog/l-and-d-podcast-guy-wallace (archived at https://perma.cc/2FJ2-QSLZ)

3 LinkedIn. LinkedIn workplace learning report, LinkedIn, 2018, https://learning.linkedin.com/content/dam/me/learning/en-us/pdfs/linkedin-learning-workplace-learning-report-2018.pdf (archived at https://perma.cc/HC68-H5GZ)

4 R Fisman. Did eBay just prove that paid search ads don't work? *Harvard Business Review*, 13 March 2013, https://hbr.org/2013/03/did-ebay-just-prove-that-paid (archived at https://perma.cc/ASX4-5N57)

14

How collaborative learning is transforming industries

Collaborative learning offers organizations a powerful toolbox for fostering the creation and transmission of knowledge in ways that can be tailored to achieve strategic objectives. Its strength as a learning modality is derived from the fact that it is not a one-size-fits-all solution and can be adapted to fit the idiosyncratic needs of an organization. In this chapter we'll examine how the movement to upskill from within through collaborative learning is transforming three very different industries – healthcare, manufacturing and business-to-business (B2B) software – to see how context shapes its implementation and outcomes. Each of these industries faces unique challenges driven by social, economic and technological change that require organizations to deploy new methods for educating and training their employees. As we'll see, collaborative learning is well suited to help organizations in each of these sectors adapt and thrive in the face of uncertainty.

Healthcare

An effective healthcare industry is vital to our wellbeing, but today this sector is grappling with unprecedented challenges in the form of acute labour shortages, changing patient expectations and technological disruption. Although many of these challenges were present prior to the start of the global Covid-19 pandemic, this historic event dramatically accelerated their development and forced healthcare organizations to explore new techniques for addressing them.

One of the most striking problems seen in the healthcare industry is a severe labour shortage, especially among floor nurses. Recent data suggests that there will be a deficit of 1 million nurses in the United States by the end of the decade, with similar shortfalls around the world.[1] There are many factors driving this shortage, including increased caseloads from an ageing population, a lack of school faculty to train new nurses, reduced operating budgets at hospitals and other healthcare organizations, and low job satisfaction scores resulting from stress and burnout. Regardless of the cause, the effects of the shortage are already having a devastating impact on our ability to access affordable and reliable healthcare in hospitals and clinics around the world, with little relief in sight.

In addition to a growing labour shortage, healthcare organizations are also grappling with workflow changes resulting from shifting patient expectations and new technologies. During the Covid-19 pandemic, for example, many healthcare organizations began offering remote patient consultations to protect both patients and staff. While telemedicine was already a large and growing trend in the healthcare sector prior to Covid-19, the use of these services has skyrocketed over the past few years. As of mid-2021, global telehealth usage was more than 30 times higher than it was immediately preceding the pandemic and roughly 1 in 5 of medical evaluation sessions occurred remotely.[2] This new method for interacting with patients required healthcare providers to rapidly adapt their services and educate staff on new technologies in order to maintain high-quality care and successful patient outcomes in an already stressful and high-stakes environment.

In the face of these unprecedented difficulties, many healthcare organizations adopted collaborative learning techniques and platforms to meet their needs. While the challenges that these organizations face are diverse and highly context-specific, they still share many features that collaborative learning is uniquely poised to address. Of particular importance is collaborative learning's ability to enable rapid reskilling, peer-to-peer knowledge transfer, identification of organizational learning needs, and measurable outcomes of learning programmes.

To mitigate the effects of the labour shortage, healthcare organizations are leveraging collaborative learning tools to rapidly train new employees and teach their workforce new skills. The first step in this process is gaining a holistic understanding of skills gaps across the organization and establishing protocols for monitoring new learning needs in response to changing conditions. Conventional approaches to learning and training are inadequate for this task because they are typically implemented in a top-down manner that may fail to address actual learner needs. Collaborative learning, by contrast, is a bottom-up approach that is designed to elicit learning needs from the learners themselves. This can take a variety of forms, such as embedded feedback systems in learning modules and employee surveys, which help L&D teams rapidly identify skills gaps and triage solutions based on the immediate needs of the organization and its patients.

Once an organization has identified its learning needs, it must create and distribute materials to address them. This has always been a challenge in the healthcare industry due to the need to balance instruction with patient care, and the labour shortage has only added to this difficulty. In this respect, the inherently peer-to-peer dimensions of collaborative learning are essential to ensuring that healthcare workers have the information they need when they need it. Organizations can draw on their internal experts to create educational content that can arbitrarily scale to meet its needs. Early career nurses, for example, often rely on the guidance of more experienced peers to become proficient in their day-to-day duties. But given the labour shortage, healthcare organizations can't afford to sideline their most experienced staff for one-on-one learning sessions that would pull them off the floor for extended periods of time. By giving their most experienced nurses a collaborative learning platform to create and share informational content with many new nurses in an asynchronous manner, healthcare organizations can ensure that their new employees have the knowledge they need to deliver safe and effective care.

Importantly, upskilling from within through collaborative learning has also proven remarkably effective at cultivating leadership among new healthcare employees, because it encourages everyone in the organization to participate in the process of knowledge creation. New employees are able to identify their own knowledge gaps and create educational content that is relevant to their peers, which helps them develop the expertise they need to become leaders in their organization as a result of the feedback mechanisms included in collaborative learning platforms.

Of course, not every employee will feel comfortable about leading a class to teach their co-workers new skills, especially if they are new to the profession and feel they lack expertise. Yet most employees have knowledge worth sharing and collaborative learning's emphasis on micro-lessons means that even new employees can share titbits of knowledge that draw on their unique strengths. This is especially critical in a healthcare setting, where employees must deal with a staggering variety of patient needs. The entire organization grows smarter when employees are empowered to share the techniques they used in a particular case, which ultimately results in improved patient outcomes.

The rapid pace of technological advancement in medicine means that healthcare workers must always be learning new skills and how to use new tools. Here, too, collaborative learning has an important role to play in fostering new competencies. A hallmark of collaborative learning platforms are micro-lessons that can be asynchronously consumed by learners. This ultimately results in an organizational culture that is centred around continuous learning. In the healthcare context, this is critically important for implementing new techniques and tools that can make a major difference in the quality of patient care.

Finally, collaborative learning offers healthcare organizations new methods for evaluating the success of their learning and training programmes. Whereas previous approaches to L&D may have focused on blunt metrics like course completion, the granularity of measurement enabled by collaborative learning platforms allows healthcare organizations to deeply understand how learning initiatives impact quality of care and the overall functioning of the organization. Improved metrics help L&D professionals in healthcare accelerate the onboarding process to mitigate staff shortages, track employee engagement to limit turnover and link specific learning initiatives to key objectives such as limiting patient readmissions through improved care.

CASE STUDY
Penn State Health

Penn State Health is a multi-hospital health system in Pennsylvania that consists of six medical centres and several additional jointly run healthcare providers. In total, the Penn State Health system encompasses 126 practices across 94 outpatient locations staffed by more than 17,000 people. It's a massive healthcare provider that delivers vital medical services to its communities; and keeping everyone on the same page through relevant learning and training programmes is no small task.

Like many healthcare organizations, Penn State Health must juggle the need to efficiently onboard new hires without constraining the care it provides for its patients. This requires efficiently using expert time to deliver the maximum amount of information to new employees with the least amount of disruption in the rhythms of the day-to-day workflow. To make it happen, Penn State Health's L&D team has crafted a four-step programme that prioritizes building experience for new hires by drawing on principles from collaborative learning.

The first priority for Penn State Health was getting a comprehensive understanding of how the organization currently learns and brings new hires into the fold. The L&D team accomplished this with a listening tour that directly engaged the employees doing work on the floor to understand their jobs, their learning needs and their perspectives on how these needs could best be addressed. Next, Penn State Health's L&D leaders mapped out the new hire journey to gain insight into how these employees enter the system and their experience during that process. They identified pain points in the onboarding process and ways to close the gap between the reality of the new hire experience and the reasons these people wanted to work for the organization in the first place. By matching expectations to reality, Penn State Health could keep employees engaged and satisfied with their work, which both improves the patient experience and mitigates employee turnover.

After embarking on a comprehensive listening tour and mapping out learning needs for new hires, Penn State Health's L&D professionals sorted through the learning needs expressed by employees to identify which competencies mattered most to the success of new employees in the organization. The goal of this exercise was to enable the team to design learning experiences that actually corresponded to the needs of new hires and their peers, rather than the L&D team's own ideas about what might work best. Once the most important core competencies were identified, the Penn State Health team was able to create programmes that directly addressed the needs of new hires to ensure they were able to grow as contributors to the organization from their first day.

Importantly, Penn State Health also prioritized measuring the outcomes of its learning initiatives. Part of this process involves administering an engagement survey to new hires to understand how they feel about their learning journey and their experience in the organization as a whole. Additionally, the L&D team works with relevant stakeholders to understand how the new hire experience shapes an employee's journey during the first crucial few months at the organization. One of the most important questions the L&D team seeks to answer is whether the employee's attitude about their training has shifted over time. If an employee felt prepared to do their job during the first few months but now feels a mounting pressure in their day-to-day tasks, the L&D team wants to understand what changed so it can create materials to help the employee be successful in their work.

The defining characteristic of Penn State Health's onboarding programme is placing individual learners at the centre of the L&D process. It's a bottom-up approach that begins by understanding the challenges and learning needs of individuals throughout the organization and how employees in different stages of their learning journey interact with one another. Rather than dictating what employees need to learn from the top, the L&D team crafts effective training materials based on the lived reality of the people who are actually working in the medical centres. By focusing on the learner and building training programmes around their needs, Penn State Health is better able to recruit and retain the talented medical professionals it needs to deliver top-notch care to its patients.

Manufacturing

Modern manufacturing is by its nature a global endeavour. It requires bringing together numerous stakeholders to procure materials, manufacture goods and deliver them to the end consumer. The problem is that the deep connections between manufacturers and global supply chains introduce several points of failure into the manufacturing ecosystem. If a manufacturer is not able to get a part for its machines or the raw materials to manufacture its goods, the entire process can grind to a halt. Given that manufacturers typically operate on incredibly thin margins and a just-in-time production model, even minor hiccups in the supply chain or on the floor can be enough to break a business. As such, it's incredibly important for manufacturers to be able to rapidly respond to changing conditions and seize every opportunity to improve performance in their organization.

The global Covid-19 pandemic brought the fragility of the manufacturing industry into sharp relief, but the challenges this sector faces have already been mounting for a number of years. One of the biggest pressures in the manufacturing industry is an ageing workforce, which is resulting in a massive skills gap. Data suggests that in the US approximately one in three manufacturing workers is over 50, which will result in a massive labour shortage over the next decade as these Baby Boomers retire.[3] Unsurprisingly, a survey of HR professionals in the manufacturing industry found that 34 per cent of them considered the ageing manufacturing workforce to be a problem and 11 per cent of them already considered it to be a 'crisis'.[4]

Addressing the challenges of the ageing workforce has two primary dimensions: upskilling ageing workers to develop proficiencies with new technologies and processes, and training a younger generation of employees to take their place. This is fundamentally a knowledge transfer problem and one that companies can solve by upskilling from within through collaborative learning. One of the main difficulties with training in the manufacturing industry is the fact that it is based around shift work on very tight timelines, which makes it hard to coordinate large-scale training sessions using conventional approaches to L&D. Collaborative learning, in contrast, is fundamentally asynchronous and is designed for self-directed learning. This means that manufacturing employees can develop the skills they need on their own schedule without disrupting the day-to-day workflow.

As the manufacturing workforce ages, the organizations in this sector risk losing a tremendous amount of knowledge when their employees retire. Collaborative learning is helping these organizations conserve their knowledge by making it easy for their experts to create content that can be shared by new employees. These individuals are able to impart a career's worth of knowledge to new employees that is guaranteed to be relevant to their job because it is developed in response to learning needs articulated by users on the collaborative learning platform. At the same time, it also helps manufacturing organizations rapidly onboard new employees, which is key to running a successful operation in this fast-paced sector.

The manufacturing industry also benefits from collaborative learning's focus on micro-lessons that can be delivered to an employee at the point of need. This is particularly important in an industry where workers are frequently interacting with complex machinery. Consider, for example, if a machine breaks on a manufacturing floor. The organization should be able to deliver the information an employee needs to troubleshoot the problem or even fix it themselves. Collaborative learning platforms enable this by providing easily accessible micro-lessons tailored to specific problems. Moreover, the employee working on the broken machine can create a small lesson based on their experience that they can share with their peers so that they are prepared to handle similar issues in the future. This kind of instruction will become increasingly relevant as more manufacturing processes become automated and require workers to develop new skills that reflect the changing dynamic between humans and machines.

Over the course of many decades, the manufacturing industry has developed and refined lean manufacturing processes that help companies stay agile and dynamically respond to unexpected changes. Collaborative learning reinforces this trend by giving manufacturing workers and organizations the tools they need to quickly learn new skills and adapt to changing conditions.

CASE STUDY

Safran

Safran is a public French aerospace company founded in 2005 that manufactures aircraft engines, rocket engines and other components for aviation and spaceflight. As the second largest aircraft equipment manufacturer in the world, Safran employs more than 76,000 people across 31 countries on four continents. Its mission is to 'contribute to safer and more sustainable aviation', which it accomplishes in no small part through a robust training programme that empowers employees to 'co-create, share, and transmit knowledge'.

In an organization the size of Safran that is tasked with creating critical flight components that help move millions of people safely around the world each year, ensuring that everyone in the organization has the information they need when they need it is key to the company's success. During the global pandemic, Safran had to rapidly transition toward flexible work arrangements that balanced needs for employee safety and business operations. At the same time, Safran was grappling with an ageing workforce nearing retirement and the rapid digitalization of its industry, which is fundamentally transforming how its employees work together to accomplish strategic objectives.

To meet its needs, Safran embraced collaborative learning techniques and tools to help facilitate the transfer and creation of knowledge throughout the company. The priority for the L&D team was developing new processes that enabled the upskilling of thousands of employees by enabling proactivity and agility in the training process. By centring learners in the training process, Safran was able to achieve its goal of training its employees faster without sacrificing the quality of the learning process.

In early 2020 the company launched Safran University as a hybrid learning programme that empowered the L&D team to deliver relevant lessons to employees anytime and anywhere. The Safran University programme allows the company to host a mix of off-the-shelf and internally developed custom content with the added flexibility of iterating on the development of training courses based on employee feedback. Safran's L&D team was able to leverage internal experts to develop rich multimedia learning modules that could be used by its distributed workforce for asynchronous 'just-in-time' training. Importantly, the development and delivery of Safran's training modules allowed its employees to participate in the learning process by commenting, reacting and asking questions about the materials.

By putting the collaborative learning process at the heart of Safran University, the company was able to ensure that employees have the knowledge they need to do their jobs effectively while meeting managers' demands for consistent training materials in a continuously changing environment. Although the tools and style of learning were new to many employees, Safran was able to achieve incredible results during the first year of its implementation. The company published more than 5,000 courses created by more than 300 subject-matter experts, which resulted in more than 136,000 hours of digital training completed. These remarkable figures demonstrate the incredible power of peer-to-peer learning to help employees thrive and companies adapt to a continuously changing environment.

B2B SaaS

B2B software-as-a-service (SaaS) is one of the fastest growing technology sectors today. B2B SaaS describes companies that develop software to facilitate interactions between businesses that were previously analogue, such as customer relationship management, marketing and procurement. The digitalization of these processes has resulted in tremendous gains in efficiency for businesses and has created a massive demand for new software products. Over the past decade, SaaS has grown into a $1.5 trillion industry that is largely driven by B2B solutions.[5] But, along the way, the sector has experienced more than its fair share of growing pains.

A hallmark of successful B2B SaaS organizations is their incredible growth rates. It's not uncommon for a B2B SaaS business to double or triple its revenue in a single year, but this parabolic growth often happens early in the company's life when it is least equipped to handle it. Sustaining this kind of growth requires B2B SaaS companies to have a relentless focus on efficient knowledge creation and transfer within the organization to meet customer needs.

Many B2B SaaS organizations provide a hands-on onboarding service for their clients to help them understand the capabilities of the software they're purchasing. The problem is that the software itself is designed to infinitely scale, but customer success professionals have only a limited amount of time in their day to onboard new clients. Collaborative learning helps overcome this disconnect by making it easy for employees to create educational materials that can be shared with new clients to smooth the onboarding process. This allows them to be more efficient with their time and focus on pain points that are specific to a particular customer, rather than rehashing the basics with each new purchase.

Collaborative learning also helps B2B SaaS organizations manage knowledge internally. Unlike on-premise software where software updates were released on a predetermined schedule, B2B SaaS products are updated continuously. This requires employees throughout the organization – engineers, salespeople, marketers and so on – to stay abreast of new changes so they can do their jobs effectively. Because collaborative learning platforms are designed to foster continuous learning, they are able to dramatically simplify the process of updating educational materials and delivering them to the relevant stakeholders in a timely manner. This ensures that everyone in the company is always aligned with the organization's vision, strategy and customer use cases.

In the wake of the global Covid-19 pandemic, many technology companies have transitioned to a fully remote or hybrid work environment, and this has created new challenges for L&D teams in these organizations. When a company's workforce is spread out around the globe, asynchronous collaborative learning tools are a must and help organizations overcome scheduling problems that are endemic to conventional approaches to L&D. Importantly, these same tools also help break down information silos that naturally arise in a high-growth software organization.

Data suggests that sales teams rarely use marketing materials when courting new customers, which results in a massive waste of effort within an organization.[6] The problem is that marketing materials are either irrelevant to salespeople because they don't address customer needs, the marketing materials are too difficult to find, or the relevant materials may not exist at all. Collaborative learning solves this problem for B2B SaaS organizations by bringing the entire team onto a single learning platform that encourages the exchange of information within and between teams. By facilitating interaction between members of different departments in the organization, collaborative learning platforms lead to the creation of content that is relevant for both internal and external knowledge transfer.

Collaborative learning also plays an important role in attracting and retaining talent in B2B SaaS organizations. Today, software organizations are locked in fierce competition for talent, which has been exacerbated by the trend toward remote work and the corresponding increase in workplace choice for employees. In this environment, the companies that are able to engage their employees the best will come out on top. Collaborative learning platforms are creating unprecedented gains in employee engagement for B2B SaaS organizations by fostering social learning environments and ensuring that employees' learning needs are met through improved feedback mechanisms. At the same time, they also enable L&D teams to better understand employee engagement levels by tracking relevant metrics beyond mere course completion rates, which allows them to address flagging engagement before it leads to an employee exodus.

In the world of B2B SaaS, speed and organizational alignment are paramount. The only way organizations can achieve high growth rates is by enabling their employees to rapidly learn and apply new information that builds toward a strategic objective. In short, B2B SaaS companies need learning tools that move as fast as they do and collaborative learning platforms are the only resource that is up to the task.

CASE STUDY
CloudBlue

CloudBlue is a SaaS company helping businesses to transform themselves by simplifying their supply chains. With its managed marketplace platform, CloudBlue makes it easier for businesses to offer subscription-based solutions of all kinds, helping companies around the world to operate more efficiently and step into new markets.

The subscription economy is an inherently complex environment, which makes it critical for every one of CloudBlue's employees to develop a depth of expertise in the company's client offerings. To do this, CloudBlue leverages its depth of internal expertise to curate great learning experiences, capture valuable knowledge and share critical insights between its teams. It also decentralizes the creation and consumption of learning experiences, working with subject-matter experts to develop and ship training content to match learner needs.

To help create these specialized learning experiences, CloudBlue draws on a range of content formats, including videos, podcasts, interviews, live events and gamified learning experiences delivered via a learning management system. This way, CloudBlue's learners can benefit from expert content delivered in a way that is engaging, diverse and compelling. This experience also helps learners to get to know other experts within the business, giving a human face to CloudBlue's learning content and making the training experience a lot more social.

CloudBlue's knowledge-sharing culture based in peer learning also makes it a lot easier for the company to cope with one of the biggest challenges in complex industries: the departure of experienced employees. By creating repositories of critical business knowledge and making these available for learners, CloudBlue can be more resilient and adaptable in the face of the disruption that comes whenever people retire or move roles. In this way, CloudBlue demonstrates one of the real values of upskilling from within: making specialist learning experiences available without having to rely on experts for synchronous delivery.

Healthcare, manufacturing and B2B software are just a few of the sectors that are being transformed by collaborative learning techniques and tools. While these industries may seem very different on the surface, and certainly have their own idiosyncratic learning needs, they are united by a need to adapt to an environment in constant flux. The world is changing faster than ever before, and modern organizations need L&D tools that can keep up with the pace. Whether it's to help efficiently onboard new employees, upskill employees to handle new machinery or manage organizational knowledge during hypergrowth, collaborative learning is the only pedagogical methodology that is up to the task. Its emphasis on decentralized peer-to-peer learning that is based on content produced by subject-matter experts in response to expressed learner needs ensures that it always delivers the right knowledge to the right people at the right time. It's a uniquely powerful learning framework that is capable of helping organizations meet a staggering variety of challenges, but it is hardly set in stone.

In the next chapter we'll explore how emerging technologies are making collaborative learning platforms even better, and how organizations can leverage these cutting-edge tools to improve L&D outcomes.

Notes

1 American Association of Colleges of Nursing. Nursing shortage, American Association of Colleges of Nursing, September 2020, www.aacnnursing.org/news-information/fact-sheets/nursing-shortage (archived at https://perma.cc/95F4-WMTV)

2 O Bestsennyy, G Gilbert, A Harris and J Rost. Telehealth: A quarter-trillion-dollar post-Covid-19 reality? McKinsey & Company, 9 July 2021, www.mckinsey.com/industries/healthcare-systems-and-services/our-insights/telehealth-a-quarter-trillion-dollar-post-covid-19-reality (archived at https://perma.cc/W3DA-3M79)

3 Society for Human Resource Management. Preparing for an aging workforce, Society for Human Resource Management, June 2015, www.shrm.org/hr-today/trends-and-forecasting/research-and-surveys/Documents/Preparing_for_an_Aging_Workforce-Manufacturing_Industry_Report.pdf (archived at https://perma.cc/A9XH-88BM)

4 Society for Human Resource Management. Preparing for an aging workforce, Society for Human Resource Management, June 2015, www.shrm.org/hr-today/trends-and-forecasting/research-and-surveys/Documents/Preparing_for_an_Aging_Workforce-Manufacturing_Industry_Report.pdf (archived at https://perma.cc/A9XH-88BM)

5 Antler Global. B2B SaaS enterprises: From inception to growth, Antler Global, 19 August 2020, https://medium.com/antlerglobal/b2b-saas-enterprises-from-inception-to-growth-734e57279c53 (archived at https://perma.cc/9Z78-BBTM)

6 A Holmes. 7 reasons why sales reps don't use marketing content, Modus, 24 November 2021, www.gomodus.com/blog/why-sales-reps-dont-use-marketing-content (archived at https://perma.cc/WHC5-7A6D)

15

The future of upskilling from within through collaborative learning

Throughout this book we've traced the origins of collaborative learning from its humble beginnings as a pedagogical technique in higher education to a paradigm-shifting force that is fundamentally changing the way organizations share and create knowledge. We've seen how collaborative learning platforms draw upon our natural inclination to learn by actively participating in the process of knowledge creation, and how this process can be supercharged by leveraging internal experts and peer-to-peer communication. We stepped inside organizations in industries ranging from healthcare to manufacturing to understand how these companies implemented collaborative learning tools to achieve strategic objectives like improved engagement, retention and customer satisfaction. My hope is that the preceding chapters have given you a new appreciation for the amazing ways that organizations and industries are already transforming by upskilling from within through collaborative learning. But this is a movement that is just getting started.

In this chapter we'll explore some of the ways that collaborative learning platforms may evolve in the future. We'll examine the impact that emerging technologies like artificial intelligence and virtual reality may have on the ways that organizations learn and how integrating these technologies into collaborative learning processes can help businesses achieve their goals and drive learner success. By taking a deep look at these trends, L&D professionals can help their organization prepare for the future and take advantage of powerful new learning tools that will define the collaborative learning platforms of tomorrow.

Artificial intelligence

There is a running joke among AI researchers that an artificial general intelligence – one with truly human capabilities – is always 40 years away. While this is as true today as it was in the 1980s, AI systems have already made significant inroads into our day-to-day lives. Every time we ask Siri a question, summon a car with a ride-sharing app, or unlock our phones with facial recognition we are witnessing the incredible power of AI in action. These examples may seem mundane, but that is exactly the point. AI is already so sophisticated and ubiquitous that we don't even notice it anymore. What used to seem like magic is now entirely commonplace.

Before we dive into how AI will shape the future of collaborative learning, it's worth taking a moment to unpack what we're actually talking about. When most people think of AI, they imagine some all-knowing machine with superhuman capabilities or what most researchers would call artificial general intelligence (AGI). By contrast, the smart applications that most of us are familiar with are actually a subset of AI systems known as machine learning algorithms. We don't need to go deep into the technical details here, but the basic idea behind machine learning is to feed a computer an immense amount of data and teach it to identify patterns in the data that it can use to make predictions. If you were building a self-driving car, for example, it's pretty important that the car understands when a pedestrian is crossing the road. To make that happen, the designers would have to feed the system millions or perhaps even billions of images of people crossing the road so that the computer can begin to identify this hazard in the real world.

In the context of collaborative learning, machine learning techniques have incredible potential for improving the way knowledge is created and shared within an organization. As we saw in earlier chapters, collaborative learning platforms require learners to voice their needs in order to work effectively. While this behaviour can be encouraged by creating a culture that is centred around learning, there are many reasons why an employee might not flag an acute learning need. Perhaps they are shy, new to the organization, or simply don't know what they don't know. A collaborative learning platform endowed with machine learning capabilities can overcome this bottleneck by automatically analysing interactions between peers and the behaviour of individual users on the platform to identify learning opportunities. If a similar question is being asked repeatedly, or multiple employees keep visiting the same portion of an internal guide, this might suggest that this is a fruitful topic for creating educational content.

One of the most promising applications of AI in collaborative learning is adapting it to the role of an expert peer. This would be similar to chatbots like Apple's Siri or Amazon's Alexa, but built into the platform itself. When a learner is working on a new skill, the AI can play the role of the expert or teacher and guide the learner on their journey. As AI improves, these interactions will have all the authenticity and depth of a conversation with a real person. While human-to-human interactions will always have a central role to play in collaborative learning, AI can help fill in the gaps when peers aren't available. This reduces the workload for everyone in the organization and helps learning occur more efficiently without sacrificing the quality or active participation of the learners. It also allows the AI system to automatically tailor learning experiences to the needs of individuals in real time. Whereas conventional educational materials are typically one size fits all, in the sense that each learner gets the same experience from a given piece of content, AI can adapt lessons and training based on the unique skills and knowledge gaps of the learner, which will both boost engagement and improve learning outcomes.

Another area where machine learning systems really shine is helping organizations manage their learning content. As a business grows, its collective knowledge grows as well, but at a certain scale it becomes too difficult for humans to manage on their own. Even with a strong search function built into the platform, it may be very time consuming for learners to find the learning content that is most relevant to their needs. This results in wasted effort through duplicated content and wasted time from searching through irrelevant materials. As an AI system comes to understand the organization's users and the learning materials available, however, it will be able to make intelligent recommendations for content that meets their needs.

For L&D professionals, artificially intelligent collaborative learning platforms will enable more rigorous measurement of learning outcomes. Machine learning works best in data-rich environments that are often far too large or complex for humans to draw insight from. This constrains what L&D departments can measure and ultimately how these measurements can be used to improve learning outcomes. But with AI in the loop, L&D teams can collect far more data points on their learners to get a holistic understanding of the impact of entire learning initiatives or individual pieces of content. When they feed this deluge of data to the machine learning system, it can identify hidden patterns and automatically produce actionable recommendations for improving content or learning processes.

All of these applications of machine learning in collaborative learning are already possible today and can be found to some degree on various platforms. But, looking deeper into the future, I see a world where humans and AI work hand in hand to create educational content on demand. We can already see a glimpse of this future in the work coming out of the non-profit OpenAI, which has developed tools like GPT-3 and DALL-E, which are capable of generating entire articles or images based on small amounts of textual input. In the future, it will be possible for AI systems to create and update entire learning modules in real time based on learner demands and the existing knowledge of an organization. This will dramatically accelerate the educational process and guarantee that learners always have the most accurate information when they need it.

Virtual reality

In Chapter 3 we saw that one of the biggest challenges facing businesses is keeping employees engaged in a world where remote and hybrid work arrangements are rapidly becoming the norm. Chat and video-conferencing tools have helped alleviate some of these pains, but during the Covid-19 pandemic many of us experienced the shortcomings of these tools first hand. A video chat is still a poor substitute for the experience of interacting with our colleagues in person.

VR systems have been of interest to pedagogical researchers since the early 1990s, when the technology was still a distant dream. Much like how asynchronous learning networks needed to wait for the dust of the dot-com bust to settle for collaborative learning platforms to truly blossom, VR was an idea that was ahead of its time but clearly held immense promise for improving the learning experience. Over the past few years, VR technologies have progressed significantly and are now capable of transporting users into lifelike virtual environments where they can interact with other people in real time as an embodied avatar. As multiple studies have demonstrated, this virtual learning environment is not only more engaging for the learner, it also improves their educational outcomes.[1]

One of the most striking findings of research on VR in learning environments is that it significantly improves information recall and reduces cognitive loads during the learning process.[2] The reason for this is because humans learn better from actively participating in the learning process. By placing learners in an immersive virtual environment, VR systems give a new depth to educational materials that simply isn't possible through the two-dimensional environment of a computer screen. This affords employees novel opportunities to engage with educational material by directly interacting with their environment and learning by doing. Importantly, because VR is an immersive digital experience, it can be tailored to the individual needs of the learner, which is crucial to effectively fill knowledge gaps without sacrificing learner engagement. As no-code VR tools continue to improve, it will be possible for anyone in an organization to create bespoke VR educational tools with the same ease of creating video or written content on collaborative learning platforms today.

As VR tools become more sophisticated they will help organizations overcome training challenges that inevitably arise in a distributed workforce. This can have many dimensions and impact employees at each stage of their journey in an organization. For example, VR tools can be used to help new hires acclimatize to a company's work processes by taking virtual tours of manufacturing floors or practising a sales pitch with a virtual customer. Companies like Walmart are already taking advantage of VR to help employees train for particularly stressful events like dealing with the Black Friday rush,[3] while the NFL is experimenting with using VR for diversity training so players and managers can build empathy by seeing what it's like to experience prejudice in a safe yet realistic environment.[4]

Virtual reality systems will be particularly important in learning contexts that involve hands-on practice, such as manufacturing or heavy industry. Organizations can create hyper-realistic simulations of machines called 'digital twins' that learners can practise new skills on before trying them in the real world. This is already being put to use in the nuclear power and aviation sectors, where risk tolerances are low and everything needs to go exactly right.[5] But it is only a matter of time before similar tools are deployed in less risky or specialized industries to improve learning outcomes by helping employees bridge the gap between theory and practice.

Arguably the most impactful feature of VR in a collaborative learning context is that it gives learners a sense of presence when they are interacting with their peers. Effective learning involves so much more than the information being conveyed – the environment, the peer group, the body language and facial expressions of the teacher all play an important role in how we retain and recall new knowledge. Unlike the relatively passive and 'flat' experience of a video call, VR systems give a new depth to learning by allowing participants to interact with each other in a three-dimensional space just like they would in real life. This enables the possibility of robust collaborative learning cultures in a completely distributed workplace by replicating the best features of in-person instruction in a virtual environment.

While VR holds immense promise for upskilling from within through collaborative learning, it is still early days for this technology. Today, most VR work environments are still low-resolution and populated with cartoonish avatars that can be more distracting than engaging. Still, the technology is progressing very rapidly and L&D professionals can expect to see an increasing number of VR systems integrated into their learning programmes over the next five to ten years, driven by the need to engage remote workers and open new pathways for learning.

Internet of Things

The proliferation of smartphones and other mobile computing devices over the past decade has led to ubiquitous wireless internet connectivity. At the same time, advances in sensor technologies and the rapidly declining cost of manufacturing computer chips have led to a proliferation of internet-connected smart devices that collectively make up the Internet of Things (IoT). The IoT revolution started with consumer electronics like internet-connected light bulbs, coffee makers and TVs, but it is increasingly making inroads into the workplace, with applications ranging from advanced manufacturing robots to safety and asset-monitoring systems.

The rise of workplace IoT systems offers a potent new tool to help drive upskilling from within through collaborative learning. One of the most promising applications is providing a fresh stream of data that can be used to identify learning needs and improve learning outcomes. IoT devices are typically endowed with a suite of sensors to capture the data the devices need to function properly. In a workplace setting, this data can provide L&D professionals with deeper insight into knowledge gaps in real time, which will empower them to address the learning needs of individual employees faster and understand whether learning materials are effective at producing desired results.

Imagine a manufacturing facility that uses a collaborative learning platform to onboard new employees. New hires are expected to take in a lot of information they need to do their jobs effectively, but even with access to a wealth of educational materials created by their peers there are bound to be gaps when it comes time for these new employees to put their learning into practice. If a machine on the manufacturing floor is connected to the internet and equipped with sensors that monitor how an employee interacts with the device, it can feed this data to an analytics platform that monitors the employee's progress as they become more proficient and familiar with their job. If a given employee keeps making a similar mistake or is not gaining proficiency as fast as their peers, the machine can automatically alert L&D professionals who can stage a timely intervention and help the employee master the skills they need to do their job more effectively.

In this respect, the Internet of Things promises to supercharge the potential of collaborative learning platforms by automating the feedback process for various job-related tasks and ensuring that no learning gaps go unaddressed. Collaborative learning platforms rely on learners vocalizing their learning needs in a timely manner so they can get the help they need from their peers and internal experts. But, as we saw earlier, there are many occasions where an employee may not feel comfortable voicing their learning needs or may not recognize a learning gap. By having an impartial digital observer built into workplace systems, L&D teams are better able to deliver relevant educational materials to learners at the time of need.

The importance of timely learning interventions cannot be overstated. Employees who do not have the educational resources they need to do their jobs effectively will quickly become disengaged from their work, which leads to low job satisfaction and high employee turnover. While current collaborative learning platforms can partially address this challenge through embedded feedback tools and a peer-to-peer approach to learning, they are still reliant on employees articulating the challenges they're experiencing. These platforms lack the data to identify situations where employees may benefit from additional training or educational materials yet have not expressed the need for those materials. By automatically monitoring employee proficiency at their job, IoT tools can help fill those gaps.

A final area where IoT systems will significantly benefit collaborative learning is by improving the ability of these systems to track and measure the outcome of learning initiatives. While modern collaborative learning platforms can offer L&D teams more robust ways to measure success than simple measurements of course completion, they are still reliant on self-reported measurements like surveys of employees and managers or relatively blunt instruments like proficiency exams. IoT devices will offer L&D professionals a rich new data stream that continuously monitors employee proficiency at their job to both track the outcome of learning initiatives and identify areas for improvement. Importantly, this data can be collected at the level of individual employees, which allows for the creation of educational material that is specifically targeted to the needs of individual workers. While big data analytics is often criticized for its tendency to turn people into mere numbers, in this case IoT does exactly the opposite and opens up the possibility for hyper-personalized educational content that is tailored to the specific needs of individuals within an organization.

Blockchain

If you've heard of blockchain technologies before, there's a good chance it was in the context of cryptocurrencies like Bitcoin. While digital money was indeed the breakthrough use case for blockchains, it is actually a class of technologies with a broad range of applications. At the most basic level, the blockchain is just a cryptographically secure digital database. It can store the same type of information as a spreadsheet or text file, but what really makes blockchains unique is the fact that they can operate in a decentralized and permissionless manner. In other words, it can guarantee perfect security over digital information without relying on a trusted third party to verify who should or should not have access to that information.

Blockchains can be a little abstract, so it's probably worth looking at a concrete hypothetical example of how they can be used in practice. Imagine you create a Google Doc that contains sensitive but important educational information about your organization. If you need to share this document with a select group of people within your organization, there are a few ways you can do that. One way is to add the names of people who can have access to the document one by one so that you have a whitelist of authorized employees. Anyone who is not on that list won't be able to access the document, but if you need to add hundreds of people or regularly update permissions, this can be a very tedious process. An alternative is simply to create a sharable link that allows anyone with the link to access the document. You can email this link to all the authorized people in the organization, but this also creates a security risk since anyone who has a copy of the link can access the document, regardless of whether they're authorized or not.

Now let's imagine that you put this document on a blockchain that is operated by your company. You can cryptographically secure this document so that only people with the relevant security keys are able to unlock it and see its contents. Although the entire organization may be able to see that the document exists on the blockchain, for anyone without the right security key it will just look like an unintelligible string of numbers and letters. It's only once they use their security key to unlock it that they are able to read its contents. The type of cryptography used by blockchains is the same that is used by intelligence agencies to store secret information, which makes it one of the most secure ways to store information.

But the benefits of blockchains go further. Blockchains can be designed to automatically execute code or give users permission to access information stored on the chain, which eliminates the need to manually update permissions for documents or other sensitive data. Furthermore, blockchains can be designed to automatically store data about how users interact with documents and other information on the blockchain, which creates an indestructible history of an organization's most important knowledge.

Blockchain technologies are a natural match for collaborative learning platforms. For starters, both are fundamentally peer-to-peer and decentralized systems. These design choices give employees within an organization the autonomy they need to act quickly without needing to wait for a sign-off from their manager or some other authority. But by combining the unique capabilities of collaborative learning platforms and blockchains, it's possible to open up entirely new applications.

For example, the ability to segment access to information to relevant departments or individual employees is relatively limited on many collaborative learning systems today. Furthermore, there are often very few guardrails in place to limit the flow of information off the platform. Depending on the security structure of the organization, it's also possible that a catastrophic data breach could result in the loss or destruction of all available learning materials. As such, most organizations are understandably wary about using collaborative learning platforms to host sensitive information, even if that information is vital for certain employees to do their jobs. This is an inefficiency that blockchains are perfectly equipped to solve.

By integrating a blockchain with a collaborative learning platform, L&D teams will be able to automatically control access to certain information in a way that guarantees that only permissioned individuals will have access to that data. At the same time, because blockchains exist across a decentralized network of computers, there is no single point of failure. So, even if a particular computer or server is the victim of a data breach, all the information stored on the collaborative learning platform – regardless of how sensitive it is – will be safe and accessible for the people who need it.

Overcoming adaptation challenges with collaborative learning

Artificial intelligence, virtual reality, the Internet of Things and blockchains are just a few of the technologies that L&D teams can expect to shape collaborative learning platforms in the years to come. These technologies offer exciting new paths for improving learning outcomes and driving organizational success, but they also introduce new challenges. For L&D professionals, one of the biggest issues will be helping workers adapt to these new technologies so they can use them proficiently and enhance their personal learning outcomes. This is especially important in industries with an ageing workforce. Older workers may find new technologies too challenging to use or simply be resistant to changing from 'the way things have always been done'.

Fortunately, collaborative learning techniques are able to help overcome the challenges that arise by integrating new technologies on collaborative learning platforms. In any organization, familiarity with any of the technologies discussed in this chapter will vary widely from employee to employee. This calls for customized learning experiences that meet individuals where they're at and help them familiarize themselves with new tools on their own terms. The peer-to-peer learning mechanisms of collaborative learning platforms coupled with tight feedback mechanisms and robust customization of educational materials allow employees to get up to speed on new technologies far faster than they would in a conventional seminar-style training.

A key to implementing new collaborative learning technologies in an organization is showing how these technologies will help everyone do their jobs better. Most people will naturally resist using new tools if they feel like they are more work than doing things the old way, which is where collaborative learning's peer-driven education system can really help. By encouraging people who are more familiar with the new technologies to create educational resources for their peers who are just learning, L&D teams can smooth the transition to these new tools by leveraging our innate proclivity to learn from others. When reluctant employees see how the new technologies make their peers' jobs easier, they will be more inclined to learn how to use them in their own work and to encourage others to do the same.

The future of upskilling from within through collaborative learning is bright and ripe with possibilities. As so often happens when making predictions about the future, reality may turn out to be very different from anything we're imagining. Just as early researchers on asynchronous learning networks could hardly imagine a world where Zoom classes and Slack chat apps are commonplace, I won't pretend that I can forecast all the ways that technology will alter the collaborative learning paradigm. What I am certain of, however, is that collaborative learning is a system built for digital tools, and as the technologies that we examined in this chapter reach maturity they will improve our ability to learn and teach in profound and as yet unimagined ways.

Notes

1 Games for Change. XR for social impact: A landscape review, Games for Change, 2020, http://gamesforchange.org/wp-content/uploads/2022/03/G4C_XR4C_2020_white_paper_Final.pdf (archived at https://perma.cc/WSE9-UMP9)

2 E Krokos, C Plaisant and A Varshney. Virtual memory palaces: Immersion aids recall, *Virtual Reality*, 2018, 23 (1), 1–15, https://doi.org/10.1007/s10055-018-0346-3 (archived at https://perma.cc/QQE3-ALVJ)

3 A Robertson. Walmart is training employees with a Black Friday VR simulator, The Verge, 1 June 2017, www.theverge.com/2017/6/1/15725732/walmart-strivr-vr-training-module (archived at https://perma.cc/G87N-QBTC)

4 M Cava. Virtual reality tested by NFL as tool to confront racism, sexism, USA Today, 10 April 2016, www.usatoday.com/story/tech/news/2016/04/08/virtual-reality-tested-tool-confront-racism-sexism/82674406 (archived at https://perma.cc/JM7Y-CW7E)

5 V Yadhav, V Agarwal, A V Gribok, et al. Technical challenges and gaps in digital-twin-enabling technologies for nuclear reactor applications, US Nuclear Regulatory Commission, Washington, DC, 2021, https://adamswebsearch2.nrc.gov/webSearch2/main.jsp?AccessionNumber=ML21361A261 (archived at https://perma.cc/2X6G-J7GQ)

Conclusion

When I launched 360Learning nearly a decade ago, the world looked very different to how it does today. The fact that this learning platform continues to drive innovation and success at my own company in addition to the hundreds of others that have joined the movement is the strongest testament I can imagine to the virtues of this approach to knowledge creation.

Make no mistake: diving into the world of collaborative learning can be frightening. To this day, many executives and L&D professionals I speak to are sceptical about upskilling from within through collaborative learning, despite its long track record of success. This speaks volumes about how deeply ingrained top-down styles of learning have become in our society. We have become so accustomed to unidirectional learning that we simply cannot imagine another way of doing something – even when the benefits are staring us in the face.

When I speak with sceptics, I am reminded of my parents asking me as a child about how I could possibly know that dinosaurs really existed just from reading a book. Who could be so credulous that they would simply take the word of someone who said that millions of years ago dragon-sized lizards roamed the Earth? The only way to know for sure was to gather the evidence I'd need to prove these assertions to myself.

The same is true for organizations that are considering upskilling from within through collaborative learning. Their executives and L&D professionals can read all the books and case studies they want, but ultimately the proof of the pudding is in the eating. The best way to understand the incredible power of collaborative learning is to take the plunge and begin applying these techniques to your own organization. It will be a slow and occasionally frustrating process. There will be unexpected challenges and failures along the way. But what I can promise you is that the struggle will be worth it.

I wrote this book with the goal of providing L&D professionals and other organizational decision makers with a guide to upskilling from within through collaborative learning. I wanted to convey both the concepts behind collaborative learning and methods for putting them into practice. A collaborative learning culture will never be fungible in the sense that it can be directly ported from one organization to another like a computer program. Each instantiation will have its own quirks that reflect the needs of a particular organization. In this sense, collaborative learning is more like a recipe from a cookery book. All the chefs that follow the recipe will use approximately the same ingredients, but each will put their own spin on the recipe to create a unique flavour.

Of course, some aspects of collaborative learning – active learner participation, peer-to-peer exchange, expert guidance – are so essential that they will be found in every organization that embraces this approach to knowledge creation. Some organizations may attempt to avoid totally relinquishing top-down control of their learning apparatus, which will result in only a partial implementation of collaborative learning. Yet, as we saw earlier in the book with the history of the first e-learning boom and bust, this is a self-defeating strategy. It is not enough to combine old ways of learning with new technologies. This will merely recreate the same old problems in a new format. Instead, upskilling from within through collaborative learning demands rethinking the learning experience from the ground up. This will involve new digital tools, but these are a means to an end (i.e. improved learning) rather than the end itself.

Failure to relinquish control over the learning process is just one of a few common failure modes that we analysed in Chapter 8. But none of these challenges are insurmountable. The important thing is to be aware of their existence and take steps to proactively avoid them. This requires a full commitment to collaborative learning throughout your organization. From the summer intern to the CEO, everyone in an organization shares responsibility for creating a learning culture. Experts and L&D professionals have an especially important role to play in this process as guides and mentors for employees who may be at very different stages in their learning journey.

Unlike conventional top-down systems of learning that are typically implemented on a defined training schedule, collaborative learning is continuous and spontaneous. Collaborative learning starts during the preboarding process and continues throughout an employee's tenure at the company. It helps new employees get up to speed faster and opens up new pathways for career advancement and self-improvement. This in turn leads to higher job satisfaction, lower employee turnover and higher employee engagement, all of which contribute to vastly improved outcomes for the organization in terms of its internal culture, customer satisfaction and bottom line.

The incredible thing about upskilling from within through collaborative learning is that it is virtually guaranteed to be successful when it is implemented in a thoughtful manner with the full support of an organization's leadership. The reason for this is because we are hardwired to learn this way. Millions of years of evolution have shown us that the most effective way to acquire new knowledge is by actively participating in its creation with our peers. We can see this in the very structure of our neurons as well as in countless experiments like Sugata Mitra's 'Hole in the Wall' experiment in India. We are collaborative learners by nature, but we need an environment that nurtures this tendency rather than attempting to curtail it.

For many organizations, collaborative learning still feels like a 'nice-to-have' feature that can drive improvements in ambiguous metrics like innovation and culture. But it won't be long before collaborative learning is a requirement for an organization's survival. Emerging challenges like remote work, employee burnout, changing media consumption habits and an ageing workforce are not going away, and companies ignore these trends at their own peril. While collaborative learning isn't enough to solve these problems on its own, it provides an important bulwark against their worst effects. And, as we've seen throughout this book, some of the most forward-thinking companies in the world have already adopted many of the principles of collaborative learning to help them adapt to our rapidly changing world.

Collaborative learning is a future-proof system that helps organizations and their employees thrive in the face of uncertainty, which is why it will eventually become the default mode of knowledge creation for every organization. Much like calling a company with a website an 'internet company' has become redundant today, eventually we'll all refer to collaborative learning simply as 'learning'. Organizations may ignore this shift, but they can't stop it. The best time to embark on your collaborative learning journey was yesterday. The second-best time is today.

ACKNOWLEDGEMENTS

This book was written with the support of David James, Daniel Oberhaus and Tom Baragwanath.

Thanks to Josh Bersin for supporting our vision for upskilling from within.

Thanks to Sangram Vajre for sharing his insights and guidance on the world of writing and publishing.

Thanks to the following L&D practitioners for taking the time to review our draft manuscript and offer valuable feedback and suggestions: Dr Hannah Gore, Adam Harwood, Andy Lancaster, Christopher Lind, Bob Mosher, Michelle Ockers, Laura Overton, Danny Seals, Perry Timms and Guy Wallace.

Thanks to AlphaSights, Busuu, CloudBlue, GP Strategies, Mitsubishi Electric, Penn State Health, Safran, ShipHawk and Slack for allowing us to tell their collaborative learning stories.

Thanks to Lucy Carter, Zexna Opara and the wider Kogan Page team for helping us bring our vision to life.

Finally, thanks to every 360Learner, past and present, for joining me on this journey and helping to make collaborative learning a reality.

INDEX

Millennial job seekers 88, 90
proto-HR functions 154–155
remote work 45–46
'user-centred resources' 21–22

vaccines 44
video-conferencing 201
virtual reality (VR) 5, 127–128, 201–203

Walmart 127, 202
Wanamaker 173

Web 2.0 12–13, 53, 54
wikis (Wikipedia) 27–28
work–life balance 50–53
World Wide Web 4–5
    see also internet
written communication (Convexity) 139

YouTube 13, 53–54

Zoom 27, 46